PENGUI

NEGOTIATE OR STAGNATE

At the impressionable age of twelve, Prakash Chugani observed customer interactions at his father's department store. That was the unwitting start to developing his understanding of negotiation skills, so much so that they would be demanded by senior executives and management students worldwide.

With a robust background in sales in his early career, Prakash led the performance of profit centres. A keen interest in propelling human excellence led him to take on the role of general manager HR at Dulsco. It was during Prakash's tenure that the company achieved the 'Great Place to Work' status.

Prakash founded Ecube Training and Consulting with a vision to empower, engage and energize individuals. His engagements have been with senior-level executives across India, the Middle East and Africa for large multinationals and local businesses.

An esteemed faculty for the negotiation and conflict resolution course at SP Jain School of Global Management, his podcast *Negotiations Paraphernalia* has been voted one of the top twenty podcasts on negotiations by *Yelp* magazine.

A practitioner of Raja Yoga meditation for over twenty-two years, Prakash hones the ability to keep a balanced mind while tackling the most complex issues.

Prakash has an MBA in marketing from the University of Missouri and an MSc in psycho-neurobics.

Negotiate or Stagnate

Have It Your Way without Showing the Highway

PRAKASH CHUGANI

PENGUIN BUSINESS

An imprint of Penguin Random House

PENGUIN BUSINESS

USA | Canada | UK | Ireland | Australia
New Zealand | India | South Africa | China | Singapore

Penguin Business is part of the Penguin Random House group of companies whose addresses can be found at global.penguinrandomhouse.com

Published by Penguin Random House India Pvt. Ltd
4th Floor, Capital Tower 1, MG Road,
Gurugram 122 002, Haryana, India

Penguin
Random House
India

First published in Penguin Business by Penguin Random House India 2024

10 9 8 7 6 5 4 3 2 1

The views and opinions expressed in this book are the author's own and the facts are as reported by him which have been verified to the extent possible, and the publishers are not in any way liable for the same.

ISBN 9780143466192

Typeset in Adobe Garamond Pro by MAP Systems, Bengaluru, India
Printed at Replika Press Pvt. Ltd, India

www.penguin.co.in

FSC
www.fsc.org
MIX
Paper from responsible sources
FSC® C016779

To my mother. She embodied the tact and skills of an able negotiator. She always got the best for herself and others. What was noteworthy is that she did it with such remarkable grace and ease . . .

and

to everyone out there who could have richer conversations, richer relationships, richer experiences and richer results

Contents

Foreword

In many places across the world, negotiating is regarded as an art form—as intricate as a Baryshnikov ballet move, as expressive as a Picasso painting and as affirming as scoring the winning goal in the football world cup.

In other places, however, as evidenced by street demonstrations, civil litigation and political dissatisfaction, there have been problems with doing the dance, reading the cues and playing the game.

Still, negotiation occurs everywhere in life. Whenever you attempt to reconcile differences, resolve disputes or manage conflict, you are playing the negotiating game. From my perspective, it's even more pervasive.

Indeed, I would say that every communication with an objective in mind is a negotiation.

So, for each of us, dealing with differences is a ubiquitous activity that adjusts and transforms relationships. It occurs when two or more parties attempt to merge their disparate points of view into a single resolution. If successful, all sides prefer the newly agreed-upon outcome to the status quo (read the old relationship) or any other mutually acceptable outcomes.

As an experienced negotiator who has also taught a course for attorneys on the subject, my book *You Can Negotiate Anything* was published in 1980. Surprisingly, it was on the *New York Times* bestseller list for nine months and was then translated into thirty-seven languages.

Although my book is still being sold, Prakash Chugani's work is a worthy successor. For he brings his unique outlook to the subject. Although of Indian nationality, he has spent more than two decades in Dubai, where he has been exposed to many cultures. During this time, he has taught and coached leadership, which in today's world is by definition a negotiation. How do you get people to voluntarily do those things that must be done?

So, for Prakash, negotiating is not a contest of wills involving pay-off demands and manipulative manoeuvres designed to maximize one's interest at the expense of the other side.

On the contrary, he sees negotiation as a dynamic problem-solving process whereby both sides interact with each other to share their real preferences, needs and interests so that mutually acceptable exchanges can be made. The result: agreements that bring 'value-added dimensions' to the relationship.

It's been over sixty years since my first book on negotiation appeared. Since then, thousands of books and articles have been written on this subject.

Amid this abundance, what is especially unique about *Negotiate or Stagnate*? First of all, it's a highly readable work.

Second, one can easily identify with the author's illuminating stories and examples. Finally, as an 'outsider', the author, like so many other immigrants, has the capacity to see what more accustomed eyes miss.

In fact, there is a Polish saying that a guest sees more in an hour than a host in a year.

For those reasons, I would recommend this book.

Herb Cohen
American negotiation expert and
author of the bestselling book
You Can Negotiate Anything

Introduction

If there is one ability that will get you whatever you want, it is the ability to make people an offer they can't refuse. At a professional level, the 'offer' could mean a promotion, a salary hike, better perks, a transfer of your preference, greater authority and more power and, at a personal level, it could mean getting your family members to accept a 'family vision and values', resolving conflicts with in-laws, your teenage children, spouse or neighbours and even something as simple as amicably agreeing to a holiday destination.

What does it take to make such an irrefusable offer? At one extreme, you need to be like Don Vito Corleone in *The Godfather*, but that would require instilling fear into others, making threats and even engaging in some bloodshed. This is not an option the sane would choose.

On the other end of the continuum is to be an able, astute and principled negotiator.

Our inability to understand the value of being a good negotiator has snatched away immense opportunities to do interesting and perhaps challenging things. Look back at your childhood days, the times spent in school, in college or even your early days at work. How many times have you refrained from participating in an activity simply because you believed that you lacked the skill or the knowledge needed? Given a second chance, armed with your current levels of maturity and experience, wouldn't you love to give those activities a go? Thus, when you look back, you were either a lousy negotiator with the self or you shied away from negotiating with others.

Every negotiation scenario is an opportunity to grow, improve, learn and achieve amazing heights. The best part is that it is not only an opportunity for one party but for all parties involved in the negotiation, provided we apply the right method. I was earlier under the impression that negotiations are battles of wits that involve aggressive behaviour, generating fear and intensifying the atmosphere with tough tactics. Due to this notion I would avoid negotiations, which has had several repercussions. As my understanding of the subject grew, I shifted my attitude and saw some remarkable results both personally and professionally. I felt that everyone should benefit from my experience and thus the idea of this book came about.

The premise of this book is based on the fact that negotiations open doors to possibilities that did not exist in the past. Its contents equip you with the right attitude, skills and knowledge so you do not miss any more opportunities. Moreover, negotiations are all-pervasive and are not just limited to corporate scenarios, and hence beneficial to all and sundry.

Knowing the impact and versatility of negotiations, everyone will benefit from learning its fundamentals. Get it right and everything is bright!

Making this book work for you

The book is intended to give the reader a good grip on negotiation and, with guided practice, they will gain mastery of it.

While every chapter builds on the previous one, the reader can flip to any page and gain valuable insights that they can apply to their day-to-day lives.

As a practice guide to hone your negotiation skills, I have provided a section titled 'Chapter challenge' at the end of each chapter. The reader is encouraged to attempt the challenge should they want to strengthen their negotiation muscle.

Chapter 1

Shifting the Negotiation Paradigm

Why Settle for Mediocrity When Excellence Is an Option?

Two sisters were arguing over an orange. The elder one said she deserved it because she was senior in age. The younger one said she should be treated with compassion and given the orange. While the argument ensued, a good Samaritan passing by overheard the conversation and pitched in to help them solve the problem. He pulled out a knife, cut the orange into two halves and gave them one half each. The sisters took their share and went their way, happy that both got a good deal. The elder sister used the rind of the orange in the Chinese tea she prepared that evening and discarded the pulp; the little sister used the pulp of the orange for the juice she was preparing and threw off the rind. What a waste!

If we do not negotiate, we settle for mediocrity

Neither the sisters nor the good Samaritan would have realized that better outcomes existed for all parties. They believed they had achieved the best deal and left satisfied. How many of us leave value on the table without even realizing it, value where both parties in the negotiation compromise? Nothing can be more disappointing than settling for mediocrity when excellence was a definite possibility. Good is the enemy of great. While it is critical to enhance our negotiation capabilities if we seek more enriched lives, the place to begin is to let go of some preconceived notions about negotiations that we may have picked up early in life. We need to challenge existing paradigms around negotiations.

Our initial encounters with negotiations were perhaps watching our parents bargaining to save a few bucks. An argument with the porter at the station to save a nickel, haggling at a provision store for a few extra grams of flour, squabbling with the domestic help over extra work that is required. Generally, anger, shame, threat and other manipulative techniques decided who had the upper hand in an argument, leaving us with a very bad taste in the mouth and leading us to conclude that we are better off without negotiations. That was unfortunately a very poor way of understanding negotiations and completely undermined its power.

At times we believe negotiations are required in certain professions such as sales, purchase and recruitment. It is not needed so much to enhance our normal lives.

My experience with negotiations, coupled with feedback from teaching Master of Business Administration (MBA) students for almost a decade now, has proven beyond doubt that when we learn to negotiate well, we begin an amazing journey of 'enrichment' on all fronts, both personal and professional.

Accessing realms of possibility

Wherever there is a conflict (clash of ideas), there is potential for negotiation and when done well, we don't simply settle conflicts, we move up accessing realms of possibilities. When we don't negotiate well, we don't only deprive ourselves of amazing outcomes, we may simply maintain the status quo or worse, things could go offhand and eventually spark unnecessary resentment.

I had recently taken over as head of human resource (HR) development after playing different stints in various other departments of the United Arab Emirates's (UAE) largest local group of companies. The director of my previous organization believed I have this three-year twitch, moving from one position or region to another every three years. I felt the best way to grow internally was to keep moving vertically and horizontally.

One of my responsibilities in the new role was to improve the engagement of our employees, around 5000 of them at that time. Previously, the HR department would conduct surveys internally, resulting in very low participation, and the entire exercise yielded dismal results. We had to bring in a sense of newness to the entire process such that it encouraged participation and made it more meaningful. I remember meeting the regional director of the Great Place to Work Institute and knew I had my answer—we would have a third party carry out an anonymous employee survey based on their world-class parameters, show us where we stand amongst the world's best and receive consultation on best practices.

In case we did have good results, our company would be ranked among the best companies to work for in the region.

When I excitedly shared the idea with our chairman, I was very surprised to find that he was quite against it. 'Let us do it the way we have in the past, Prakash. I am more comfortable with that.' I was given to understand from my colleagues that others had tried in the past to engage reputed external consultants for the same, but our chairman just refused to go in that direction.

I revisited my chairman the next day and stated that I felt engaging the consultant was an idea that had quite gripped me and that I wished to understand his inhibitions. Initially, he seemed extremely reluctant to divulge his feelings and tried to convince me that we had all the capability to do it in-house, but when I persisted, he opened up. He told me that an external consultant could get hold of some sensitive information which might be shared with others. Second—and that seemed to be the real problem—in case we were surveyed and we did not make it to the list of best companies, it would be quite a loss of face for us—we being one of the oldest companies in the region. I was already given assurances of confidentiality and that in case we did not make it to the list, no one would even know that we had participated. I told him that we need not worry about it and that this time things would be different.

We had some months before the survey and initiated various steps and introduced thorough systems in support of our employees. We noticed positive shifts that fostered great responses from our clients. We conducted our survey, received invaluable inputs and best practices to enable our people and finally, we were pronounced as a 'great place to work' in the UAE, ranking at number 8. Our employees' branding skyrocketed, our reputation as an organization went up a few notches and, internally, our employees were excited beyond belief. Our chairman was extremely pleased and hosted a special company-wide celebration. It was the beginning of immense growth in all directions for our company.

During the festivities and merrymaking, my thoughts drifted back to the moment when I negotiated with my chairman. A key success factor was understanding the **chairman and looking beyond his immediate response, getting to the root of the problem and finding a clever way to navigate**. In return, we were given the opportunity to do what we felt would boost our company's growth. The rest was win, win, win and nothing less than win for all stakeholders.

You don't get what you deserve, you get what you negotiate

There are so many times when I have defaulted on my credit card, where I have simply forgotten to pay up on time. Invariably I am penalized with a late fee and a finance fee. I call the agent as soon as I know this, and every time I have asked them to reverse it, they have. I remember once I had overlooked it and paid for it. When I called them, they refused to reverse it since I had already paid up for it. 'Sir, if you had called us earlier, we would have definitely reversed it, but since it has been paid, the system now will not allow for a reversal.' The words of writer Chester Karrass hit me so hard, and I realized it so very well—you don't get what you deserve, you get what you negotiate.

Sometimes we hesitate to ask or wait so long for an opportunity that we miss the bus. What is the worst that can happen when we ask? We might be rejected. **It's better to be rejected than to live with the regret of never having asked because you technically deprived yourself of a 50 per cent probability of a 'yes'.** Knowing that perseverance conquers all, when rejected, we need to creatively change our approach and try once again. There are so many times in the past that I simply kept quiet withholding something that I wanted thinking I might look stupid asking. Simple things like hesitating to ask the flight attendant for an extra cup of coffee, or requesting a passenger to exchange seats, or checking with someone if they wanted me to assist them with their luggage—all I had to do was ask.

Only by negotiating can we achieve a win-win

The possibility of a win-win will never happen if we don't negotiate. Win-win states that we can both achieve our outcomes, if we were to sit across the table and negotiate, openly. I have unfortunately witnessed so many occasions when people have compromised, let go of their share and even withdrawn without any closure simply because they haven't negotiated in its true spirit. Win-win thinking makes amazing things possible.

My nephew and niece would constantly fight over who would get the front seat of the car, next to the driver. The fights were getting a little too much to manage. My brother tried explaining that they could take turns. But the trips varied by distances, hence the plan did not work. Eventually, he got them to agree that whoever lets go of sitting in front gets to manage the music system. That day on, the fighting stopped, and harmony was restored.

Every existing business has come to the realization that seeking a win for all its stakeholders is the way to thriving—a win for their clients, the society and their shareholders. Even while innovating, the first step in Design Thinking is empathy, i.e. a deep understanding of the needs of the end user. In other words, the only way my product or service will win is when I try to help the end user win. 3M, IBM, Uber, Airbnb and Amazon are classic examples of negotiating a win-win and hence succeeding beyond measure.

Case in point: being end-user centric helped a team at IBM use insights generated from a wide-ranging study of human interaction to transform that ubiquitous marketing event, the trade show, into a collaborative experience.[1] Instead of a critique of the new model by the management hierarchy, the design team prototyped and tested it with real customers.

Essentially, if I want excellence over mediocrity, more from life and to achieve a win-win, ***both within corporate settings and in everyday situations****, negotiation is a key skill to master. No wonder Negotiation Skills is the most popular course at the Harvard Business School.*

Conclusion

Negotiation and excellence go hand in hand. A lot is left on the table when we do not negotiate, and this usually results

---

[1] Jeanne Liedtka, Andrew King and Kevin Bennett, *Solving Problems with Design Thinking: Ten Stories of What Works* (Columbia Business School Publishing; Illustrated edition (2013).

in a lose-lose for both parties. Shifting your attitude and perception about negotiations from something that poses obstacles to something that creates opportunities will take you a long way in life.

Chapter challenge: Paper-clip exchange

A good way to begin developing any skill is by getting an insight into where you already are at this juncture. The 'Paper-Clip Challenge' will show you where you stand and also suggest areas of development.

Step 1: Take a paper clip and think of the various ways in which it can be used. Find someone who you believe may find it useful and valuable. Convince them to exchange the paper clip for something (material) that you believe has a much higher value.

Step 2: Whatever you have received from this person in exchange for the paper clip, exchange that with another person for something of a higher value.

Final Step: Whatever you have received from the second person, exchange that with a third person for something of a higher value.

If you were able to do this with ease, pat yourself on the back. Even if you found it tough, you deserve a pat for taking up the challenge. Once the 'pats' are done, process the learning at two levels. First, how different people perceive value. Hence, if you can position what you have as valuable to them, they are willing to act in your favour. Second, consider the infinite possibilities of continuing the challenge many times over. You start off with something of really low value monetarily and land up with something of unbelievably high value.

By the way, author Kyle MacDonald testified to this by bartering his way from a single red paperclip to a house in a series of fourteen online trades over the course of a year.[2]

[2] 'From Paper-Clip to House in 14 Trades,' CBC News, 7 July 2006, https://www.cbc.ca/news/canada/from-paper-clip-to-house-in-14-trades-1.573973.

Chapter 2

Negotiation Navigator

Mastering the Art of Effective Deals

The significance and versatility of negotiations can be easily underestimated. We find negotiations in every nook and corner, including places most unexpected. A copywriter whose daily walk to work takes him past a blind beggar on a street corner. His signboard reads, 'I'M BLIND. PLEASE HELP.' Every day, the beggar is largely ignored by the passers-by.

When someone neutral sees the beggar being ignored, they could hold the belief that people are not willing to part with their money, they are selfish, they don't care and so on.

One sunny morning, the copywriter stops, takes out a marker pen, scribbles three words on the signboard and then moves on. From that day, the blind man's cup is stuffed with notes and overflowing with change. The copywriter has adapted the signboard to read: 'IT'S SPRING AND I'M BLIND. PLEASE HELP.'

Same people, same setting; all that shifted was the perspective of the passers-by and the beggar raised his 'negotiability'.

When we fail to understand that effective negotiations have the power to give us the results we want, we blame everything around us for our failures. That is not a very nice space to be in, both psychologically and practically. We could become very reactive rather than proactive. **As we embark on the learning journey of negotiation skills, it is thus very important for us to come to terms with its power and ubiquity**. This will motivate us to learn to excel in the subject with greater sincerity.

In what areas would I negotiate?

Far from popular belief, negotiation is not confined to mainstream selling. It happens across all levels and ages, and for all reasons; on the streets, in boardrooms and in the cozy living rooms of our homes. Here are a few examples to prove this.

When driving

Navigating on a twelve-lane driveway in the Emirates or weaving through the busy streets of Mumbai requires one to constantly decide on speed, lane, overtaking, indicating, type of vehicle to use and so on. Even a simple event of driving on a road has so many things to negotiate!

When conveying bad news

A man was told by an astrologer that he would die before his elders. The astrologer was rebuked and rejected. The astrologer thereafter started telling people, 'You will outlive your ancestors,' and they expressed their wholehearted gratitude.

When seeking permission

Two disciples were having an argument around when they were allowed to smoke. The first one said that he was strictly forbidden by the master to smoke while praying. 'I specifically asked him if I could smoke when I am praying and Master bluntly refused,' he quipped. The second disciple said that the master granted him permission. 'I specifically asked him if I could pray when I am smoking and Master gladly agreed.'

In war situations

To me, a war is a case of 'failed negotiations'. I don't think we would ever go to war if we had faith in negotiations and persevered.

When putting a child to bed

Some of the most difficult negotiations are those that we have with children, be it putting a toddler to bed or establishing curfew timings with teenagers. Very often, our inability to negotiate makes us blow our tops. That is unfair in any negotiation. We should stay calm and composed. Only then can we have access to the best ideas and foster positive relationships. Stay on course of the conversation, without quitting or losing patience. Your behaviour today will decide how your kids manage conflicts and how the two of you interact in future.

When resolving disputes

A dispute arises when there are conflicting interests within an organization or society. But when understood in the right spirit and tackled sensibly, a dispute can be exceptionally beneficial to all involved, ensuring maximum productivity for organizations and high levels of well-being for members of the society. For example, the manager delegates a job to their direct report and demands that it be completed in two days. The direct report has other important jobs to complete over the next two days and explains to the manager that it will not be possible to complete it in two days without compromising on the other jobs. They eventually agree to complete it in four days. The manager reflects on this event and realizes the tight spot they are in and begins developing other direct reports who had extra time on their hands. The result: a much stronger team with enhanced capacity and capability.

When negotiating with the self

This happens non-stop. The mind is constantly engaged in planning, prioritizing, decision-making, executing, persevering and so on. To be a great negotiator with the self, it is important to develop the art of 'clearing the space' from time to time. This way you have a clean slate to place your options and to make sensible decisions on. As we continue to explore ideas and insights on negotiation, we will see how this art supports us in getting amazing results, both for ourselves and for others too.

Negotiations in corporate

Studies show that good negotiation skills play an important role in your success as a corporate executive and your potential for advancement.

Being a good negotiator allows you to build, maintain and improve workplace relationships, which is an essential part of being a successful manager and leader. It helps achieve important goals and gets you what you need and want for yourself, your department as well as your organization. Efficiency is another benefit that comes with being a good negotiator. Instead of spending hours arguing with people and trying to force them to do what you want, you can reach agreements, find solutions to tough problems, and keep work moving ahead more easily and with less effort.

Here are a few instances where negotiation is vital:

Asking for a raise/promotion: Everyone knows that negotiation skills are crucial when it comes to asking for a raise or a promotion. Considering its impact, we have an entire chapter dedicated to negotiating at the workplace. While we are at it, let me share a personal anecdote on this front.

At the start of my career in the UAE, I was working as a sales executive in the Waste Management Division of our company. I was doing my MBA simultaneously and once I graduated, I had a meeting with my manager, an English gentleman, and conveyed my intention for a promotion. I followed that up with a formal letter describing the subjects I had learnt and what I was capable of managing, thus soliciting higher responsibilities. (As the letter was written powerfully, I have dissected it in the chapter on communication.) We went back and forth with opportunities available in the group of companies, and the following month I was promoted three levels up to a manager with profit and loss (P&L) responsibilities for an entire region.

Selling: Success in sales does not come from hard selling, i.e. pushing the product down the customer's throat, but from consultative selling (understanding their needs and fulfilling them with the product/service). Negotiating in sales is all about selling consultatively, which is the best way to ensure a long-term relationship with the client and to foolproof yourself against competition.

Purchasing: This is a function that is often taken for granted as we believe it is easier to buy than to sell. However, when quality, time and reliability are of top priority, including the cost, of course, this function is of utmost importance to the organization, and hence, we need to negotiate in such a way that we win while our vendor wins too.

Recruiting: A good recruiter must be a star negotiator through the entire cycle of recruitment. Getting the candidate to agree to the job role and remuneration is one part, another crucial part is to convince the hiring manager as to why this candidate ought to be chosen, and sometimes even paid extra. I remember convincing a candidate to take a job for a position one level less than what he had applied for and for a salary 10 per cent lesser than was advertised because of an internal botch. I was able to show him why it would benefit him to do so with solid evidence. He took it up and today he still works in the same company and is very well placed.

Changing a policy: While policies form the framework of any company, they can restrict growth and progress if they remain inflexible. 'We would love to help you, but it's against company policy.' This is one of the most irritating statements I have ever heard. Painful to see the tail wag the dog.

As employees in organizations, when we see that policies need to change, we need to present a valid case. When I was planning to change the way our company approached 'performance management', I had to first bring in an expert from a leading bank in Abu Dhabi to share his insights with our CEO and leadership team, and then present what we had in store. My ideas were readily accepted. Negotiation is also about planning how, when and where to place your cards so you have a deal that is a winner.

Building and leading teams: It takes immense effort, focus and discipline to build a great team and to keep it moving ahead towards the organizational goals. There is a mutual dependence between the leader and the team and demands from each other could be conflicting. A good leader understands and even encourages these conflicts to be openly aired and finds ways to have them amicably resolved. As a great negotiator, one never shies away from conflict but understands its importance and facilitates a good outcome from it.

Conclusion

Keep your ears to the ground—opportunity for excellence is scattered all over. Don't worry if you miss one, be alert to pick up the next one.

Chapter challenge: Short-change no more

Consider two recent situations from your life—one personal and another professional—where you felt short-changed. What did you do and what did you not do to get those results? How do you think an effective negotiator would have tackled these situations? Journal your thoughts and ideas and highlight your greatest learning from this exercise.

Chapter 3

Beyond Mediation

Design a Foolproof Master Plan

During my workshops, I ask students to list out the competencies of negotiators, i.e. for a negotiator to be successful, what are the traits/competencies they must possess. The usual list looks something like this:

Effective speaking	Respect	Creativity
Effective listening	Self-confidence	Patience
A sense of humour	Emotional intelligence	Preparation
A positive attitude	Persistence	Presence of mind

There is one aspect that is mostly overlooked and yet remains the most critical: BATNA. Every great negotiator must possess a BATNA, which would to a large extent decide how the negotiation goes.

BATNA stands for Best Alternative to a Negotiated Agreement. It is the best alternative should your negotiation fail. In other words, if you are unable to achieve the expected outcome with the other party, what alternatives do you have . . .

In Neuro-Linguistic Programming, we have a similar concept called the Law of Requisite Variety. It states that the system/person with the most flexibility of behaviour will control the system. It basically means that the more choices you have, the more freedom you can experience and the better the quality of life you can have.

The three most important words in negotiations are **prepare, prepare and prepare**. Failing to prepare is preparing to fail and one big mistake many make is to not spend enough time preparing for negotiations. A step that simply cannot be overlooked if we are seriously considering great outcomes from the negotiation. BATNA is all about preparations.

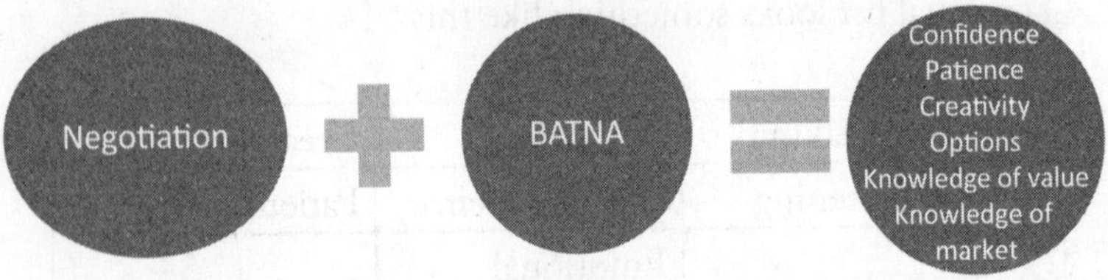

BATNA in our day-to-day life

Asking for a raise

You could expect two eventual outcomes when you approach your superior for a raise: they will either agree (with or without conditions) or they will disagree. Before you head to the negotiation table, it is critical to go prepared with what outcome you are willing to settle for, and in case you do not have that, what would you do. In their book *Getting to Yes*, one of the most renowned books on negotiations, Roger Fisher and William Ury ask this important question: when negotiating a raise, what is a better option—a gun in the pocket or an offer letter from another company? Your BATNA is really strong when you have an offer letter from another company because in that case, you know what your best alternative is if this does not go well. Hence, regardless of whether or not you go with that alternative, you go into that negotiation with confidence. Your confidence will immensely favour you in that negotiation.

Buying something

Before purchasing my second-hand SUV, I prepared well before the face-to-face with the owner. I ensured I had suitable offers from other credible owners, including the authorized car dealer. I was absolutely confident with the market rates for similar vehicles, and genuinely could walk out of this deal and take up any other offer from the other owners, although they were a tad lesser in terms of my preference. When I walked into the negotiation with the owner, an American ophthalmologist, he sensed my confidence from the word go. He knew I had done my homework and had suitable alternatives. He offered me his lowest price within minutes. It was almost 20 per cent less than his 'non-negotiable' initial offer. We closed the deal and I am today the happy owner of a reliable and beautiful SUV!

Selling something

The BATNA of a salesperson is their pipeline.[3] If they have a very slim pipeline, they will be ready to accept anything from the client. On the other hand, if they have a strong pipeline in place, it would establish a sense of confidence and balanced judgement, so that they do not give in to a poor deal in desperation. A robust sales pipeline indicates the salesperson has various alternatives or BATNAs available to them in case a particular deal does not materialize.

Leading teams

Through coaching, mentoring and training, CEOs are able to develop the leadership capability of their entire team. When every individual in the team develops and betters their leadership capacity, the CEO creates a strong BATNA. They are not dependent on a single team member but can draw on the expertise of any member on their team, hence wielding enormous power.

If you don't have a BATNA, create one

Some may believe that they do not always have a BATNA when they go into a negotiation. While this may be true, it is not enough to rest on our laurels and make this an excuse not to 'create' one, especially when the negotiation is important for us. I was holding an account in a bank where I was not given proper service or advice on my investments. I visited

[3] A sales pipleline contains leads that trickle down from a 0 per cent chance of closure (unqualified) to a 90 per cent chance of closure

the bank and spoke to the personnel there but received a very poor response. I wanted to meet the manager and let her know that I wasn't getting the service I expected. I had no BATNA so I had to create one. I visited another branch of the same bank and spoke to them. I found their service to be satisfactory and so expressed my desire to transfer my funds across. They assured me that it wouldn't be a problem and that it would take them just two working days to get the new account activated. I only had to fill out a form. In less than an hour, I received a call from the manager of the original branch, requesting I meet her when I was free. I visited her and she wanted to know why I was changing my branch, so I shared my plight. From that day to today, I have direct access to the bank manager and receive service par excellence.

The following two scenarios illustrate possible outcomes when negotiating with and without a BATNA.

Scenario 1: Negotiating without a BATNA

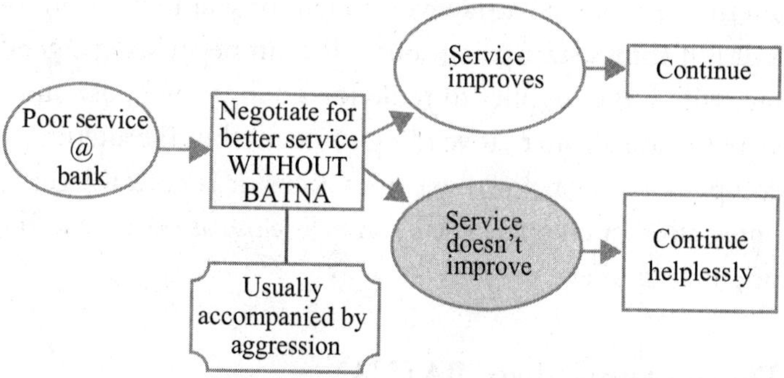

Scenario 2: Negotiating with a BATNA

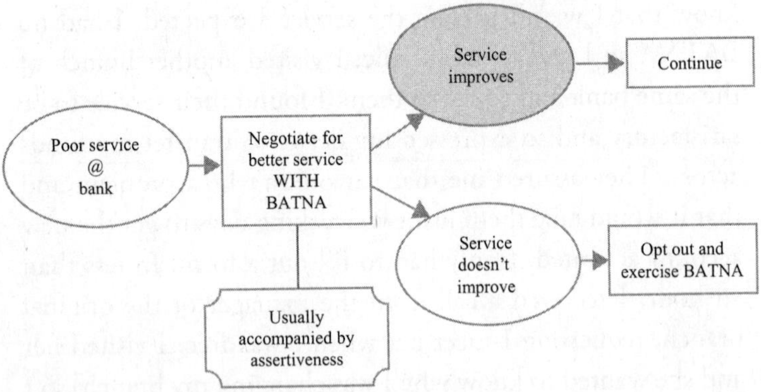

A weak BATNA is worthless

It is important to remember that a BATNA can be strong or weak. Once we have a BATNA, it is also crucial for us to strengthen it, if we feel it is weak.

Strengthening the BATNA could mean looking for alternatives that are attractive enough for you to walk out of a deal if things start going south. If I am negotiating a good rate with a tile supplier to retile the floor of my house and I were to have an alternative tiling company, but the alternative company is way below my expectations, it is crucial I get to know another company that comes as close as possible to the original supplier.

Do you know 'their' BATNA?

We have seen how important it is for anyone as a negotiator to have/strengthen their BATNA. It is equally important to anticipate the BATNA of the other party. What is their alternative in case they don't get you to agree to their terms? Doing so will get you to play your cards astutely. Should you understand that their BATNA is weak, you are in a fantastic position to have a really favourable deal, else you may leave quite a bit on the table.

Our company was awarded the contract to supply tank cleaners to the owners of a double-bottom oil tanker. When we got onboard the vessel at Fujairah Anchorage and started the job, we noticed that we had massively underestimated the quantity of sludge and hence would suffer a loss doing that job. Besides, we knew that because of the quantum of work involved, we would take an additional week to complete the job. I had to quickly find a way to get the best for both parties. I reported to the superintendent of the vessel that considering the quantity of the sludge, we would need an extra week to complete the job, and if the job has to be completed on time, then I would like to have a meeting with the owner at the earliest. I was aware that the owner would not be in a position to mobilize additional manpower and for every day that his vessel gets delayed, he would pay an additional $15,000 per day. Besides, there would be a huge opportunity cost that he would have to bear for the delay.

In two days, the owner flew into the country and we men onboarded his vessel. I first shared with him the fact that we misfired on the quantity. We were willing to take a hit, but we would have liked to support the owner by beefing up our manpower and equipment, by doing so we would be able to complete the job as scheduled. We would need an additional $25,000 for this. In case he refused, we would maintain the status quo and as per our contract, we would complete the job, but there would be a delay.

As I was aware of the BATNA of the vessel owner and knew that to compensate us with that amount would save him hundreds of thousands, and that anyone sensible would take the offer, I was confident with my stand. Within fifteen minutes of my making the proposal, he signed the additional worksheet agreeing to the new fees. We went back to the drawing board, boosted our resources and completed the work on time.

Conclusion

Going to a negotiation without a BATNA is equivalent to going to war unarmed. In other words, failing to plan is a definite plan to fail. BATNA is the negotiator's proverbial 'Brahmastra', which no human power can defeat!

Chapter challenge: Strategy before execution

Prepare for an upcoming negotiation, either at home or at the workplace. It could be a product or service you are looking to buy/sell or a relative you want to convince for something. Our usual stance would be to make an approach and then based on the response, we play our next card. Now, even before you enter any negotiation, conjure and strengthen your BATNA. Do whatever it takes to have a strong BATNA and then approach the negotiation.

Chapter 4

The Negotiation Blueprint

Building Win-Win Solutions

How many times have we made a purchase only to return home and realize that we have spent way more than we had anticipated. We may have been carried away by the sales pitch, a higher version of the product or something that seemed much better but caused us to pay way too much for it. We realize after the purchase, *OMG, I could have really done well with the basic model that served me perfectly well rather than the upgraded one.* Why does this happen?

I have mentioned earlier the importance of preparation before entering any negotiation when we spoke about BATNA. Another critical component and calculation that we must make way in advance is to know at what price would we walk out of a deal, i.e. what is the bare minimum we are willing to accept as a seller and what is the maximum we are willing to part with as a buyer.

I have noticed that smart negotiators do tend to nibble away as much as they can, periodically. For example, they would first ask for a discount of, say, 5 per cent. Once you agree, they would then ask for an extension of credit by another thirty days. Once you agree, they will then have the delivery terms changed, and so on and so forth. When we add up all of these seemingly small allowances, we realize we would have been better off with 'No Deal'. Therefore, before entering a negotiation, the limits must be crystal clear. This is called the 'Walk-Away Price', a least or most someone is willing to accept depending on whether you are a seller or buyer.

Who should know your Walk-Away Price (WAP)?

How many times have we heard people ask: is this your last price? This is a killer question, at least at the start of any negotiation. It actually kills the negotiation. When you pose such a question, you leave the other party with two choices: either they say 'yes' and then leave them no room for any further negotiations or they say 'no', which makes them look foolish because if you had a better price, then what are you waiting for, blurt it out! Any smart negotiator would keep their WAP to themselves and they know that the other party would keep their WAP to themselves.

Anticipate the WAP of the other party

A good negotiator will also anticipate the WAP of the other party, and will finalize the deal at a price that is as close as possible to the other party's WAP. This step is critical, and I will cite an example where not doing this well could be dangerous.

A property owner was looking to sell a substantial piece of land in Manchester. As per the market rates for residential properties, he valued the land at $10 million although he was willing to go down to $8.5 million. He eventually found a buyer who was willing to pay him $10.5 million. He soon closed the deal and was thrilled. He later realized that the buyer got grants from the government and used the property for commercial purposes. Had he known this earlier, he could have fetched at least another $5 million. In fact, the buyer of the property was willing to go all the way up to $18 million for this property. He knew that since the market rate for residential properties was near the $10-million mark, he tried his luck and immediately closed the deal. If only the seller had any clue about the WAP of the buyer, the dynamics would have been so different!

Zone of Possible Agreement (ZOPA)

The range between the WAP of the seller and the WAP of the buyer is called the Zone of Possible Agreement (ZOPA). If I were to cite the example quoted earlier for the land in Manchester, the seller's WAP was $8.5 million and the buyer's WAP was $18 million. The deal could have been closed anywhere between $8.5 million and $18 million. If the buyer was a strong negotiator, he could have closed it close to $8.5 million and if the seller was stronger, he would have closed it close to $18 million. The deal, however, cannot be closed at a price beyond this range as that would fall beyond the WAP of the parties. This range is called ZOPA and through negotiations, both the buyer and seller are trying to ascertain the ZOPA.

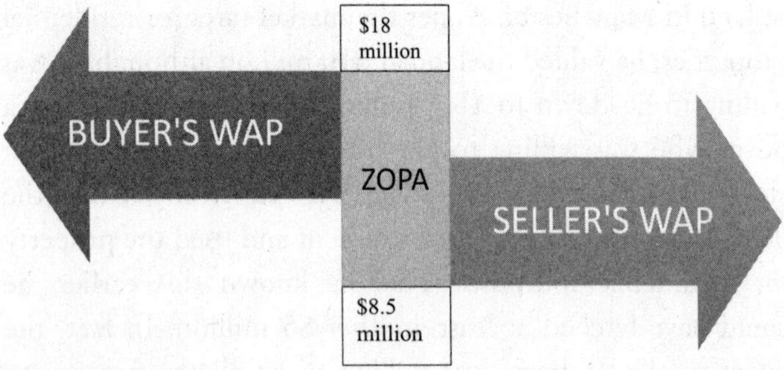

Estimating the WAP of the other party

This is where negotiations become more scientific and are not mere verbal gymnastics. We must enter into a negotiation after thorough research, study and analysis. Sometimes, the opening offer is usually very high just to gauge the response of the other party. If it seems quite dramatic, we realize we have gone way beyond their WAP and if they seem comfortable, we may have hit it on the head!

Definitely, it also would require us to pose appropriate open-ended questions to the other party and then to listen for a 'non-response'.

What is a non-response? Many a time, the other party would not like to blatantly lie. So let's take the example of the Manchester land deal case once again. The seller may ask the buyer: what do you plan to do with this property? The buyer may not directly lie but would say things to cover the truth.

'Well, I am not so sure . . . I would plan post this deal. There are several options and I am going to weigh them based on the demand.' If we ask a question like, 'Will you be using it for commercial purpose or residential purpose?' he might say, 'Our company has had immense success in the residential business and hence we don't see any immediate reason for us to do otherwise.' Notice that the buyer does not lie. Unless I am listening actively, I will not pick up the 'non-response', where the party is avoiding giving me a direct answer. You need to probe further in this case: 'So should I take that as a yes, no or maybe?' Then, let him know that we will have a clause in the contract stating that if he uses it for commercial purposes, then there will be a 50 per cent hike in the price. That way, the seller is covered.

There are similarly other ways to estimate the WAP of the other party. What I do is to check with other vendors, speak to my contacts to understand what they would pay for similar services and get some idea of the market. I then take it that there is a profit and overhead built into what the market is offering and thus when I am negotiating, I am not completely in the dark. It may sound very logical, but it is a step that can be easily overlooked.

I remember wanting to get my residence in Chennai repainted and since I was quite new to the town, I did not have much idea of the market. I received an offer from a contractor to do my house and when I asked for the breakdown, he specified the daily rate for painters. I negotiated and got a discount of approximately 10 per cent.

While I found the overall price to be reasonable, I decided to run this past a close friend who lived in the same town. When I sent him a WhatsApp message, he instantly called me and suggested that I was paying almost 30 per cent more. He broke down the daily wages for me and I could see for myself that I had been taken for.

I called the contractor and told him that I wished to hire the workers on a daily-wage basis because I would save a huge amount. I let him know, with evidence, what the market was charging, and he asked me to hold on for a day. He called me the following day and agreed to reduce his price by an additional 25 per cent and promised some extra polishing for the wooden furniture at home.

We could see how the concepts of WAP and ZOPA are useful at home when negotiating with a teenage son or daughter. The usual curfew time is 9 p.m., but your teenager wants a special extension on a particular weekend. If push comes to shove, as a one-off, you can extend the curfew to 12 a.m. (your WAP). Your teenager knows that they must be out until 10 p.m. (their WAP) but would love to push that further up. Our ZOPA will fall between 10 p.m. and 12 a.m. If your teenager is a better negotiator, they may get to extend the curfew to 11.45 p.m. and above, and if you are a better negotiator, you will have your teenager happily agree to anything less than 10.30 p.m.

Who should make the opening offer?

At the outset, drawing from a wealth of negotiation research, as a negotiator, you must make the first offer. The primary reason for this is that the one who makes the opening offer usually 'anchors' the negotiation, i.e. all negotiations now begin at a very subconscious level from that point. Research by Amos Tversky and Daniel Kahneman (1974) shows that humans do not necessarily make decisions rationally.[4]

Having said that, while making the opening offer, you must be well informed about where your offer is coming from rather than shooting from the hip. So, if you believe you have enough information about the WAP of the other party, the market rates and other dynamics, then you must make the opening offer.

Anchoring

Effective negotiators influence the other side's perception of the set of possible outcomes, the Zone of Possible Agreement (ZOPA). When appropriately used, the opening offer serves as an *anchor*, often dramatically changing the other side's perception of your reservation price and hence the ZOPA.

Brian C. Gunia, professor at Kelly Business School, has researched the topic of anchoring and published several articles to support its importance in negotiations.[5] To help us understand the subject better, he has cited an example similar to the one below.

Deepa and Emad are negotiating over the sale of a laptop. Deepa, the seller, is willing to take anything over $1000.

---

[4] Amos Tversky and Daniel Kahneman, 'Judgment under Uncertainty: Heuristics and Biases: Biases in Judgments Reveal Some Heuristics of Thinking under Uncertainty', *Science* Vol. 185, No. 4157 (27 September 1974), pp. 1124–31.

[5] Brian Gunia, *Responding to Another Negotiator's First Offer* (Harvard Business Publishing, 2017).

Emad, the potential buyer, is unwilling to pay over $1500 for the laptop. Of course, both Deepa and Emad know their own walk-away prices, $1000 and $1500, respectively, but are uncertain about the other side's walk-away price.

Emad asks Deepa to make the first offer. Deepa guesses that Emad is willing to pay at least $1250 for the laptop, and may be willing to pay as much as $1550. She does not want to make an offer that is too outrageously high, since Emad might be insulted and walk away from the deal altogether. Thus, she offers to sell Emad the laptop for $1600.

Prior to the first offer, Emad had not thought much about Deepa's walk-away price. Emad's entire focus is now on Deepa's offer, only $100 higher than his walk-away price. After a little thought, Emad guesses that Deepa's walk-away price is somewhere around $1500. Emad tentatively counters with $1350.

The bargaining continues: Deepa counters with $1500. Emad counters with $1400, and Deepa offers to 'split-the-difference': $1450. Emad accepts and is happy.

The deal closes in favour of Deepa, and the main reason is that she made the opening offer and anchored the negotiation from that point, which was close to Emad's walk-away price.

When the other party makes the opening offer

While we understand that negotiations are anchored to the opening offer, how can you counter an opponent's opening offer? Let us understand the various options and see what the best way is to respond to each of them.

a. The opening offer of the other party is bad:

You have a product and are willing to sell it for $3000. The other party opens the offer with $1000, which is a terribly bad offer. Which would be your best response?

1. It has been a pleasure knowing you. Let us stop all negotiations and part as friends.
2. What! That's ridiculous. How dare you undervalue my product so much?
3. Tell me where did you get the $1000 from? On what basis have you stated that?
4. Looks like this negotiation is going to last a very long time.
5. Seems like you have just read the bestselling book on 'star negotiators'.

The first two answers are typical of an amateur negotiator. Reacting rather than responding. Becoming a victim of emotions rather than being a victor. This will only end in a 'no deal' and that is not the aim of this negotiation. The third option is a common one used by many, which is also a poor response because it forces the other party to justify where they are coming from and therefore digging them deeper into their initial position. The last two options are good responses and let us understand why research recommends these.

When they make a ridiculous opening offer, we simply deflect it in good jest, and research says that we do that by trying to bring in some humour. 'Looks like this negotiation is going to last a very long time' instantly lightens the atmosphere and attempts to dilute the ridiculous offer made by the party while letting the other party know that I am aware of what is happening. In other words, we completely disregard what the opening offer was and hence throw the anchor off balance. Once we do so, we then put forward our offer.

b. The opening offer of the other party is good:

Continuing from the earlier example, you are willing to sell your product for $3000 and this time the other party offers you $3200—an offer that is too good to be true. How would you respond?

1. Okie dokie. We have a deal.
2. Well, appreciate your offer. I was hoping for something a bit better than that. How about an additional 10 per cent and it's a done deal!
3. Hey, don't you think you are offering me bit too much? Let's close it at $3000 and we are good.

The majority go for option 1. Let's grab the great offer with both arms. You reveal too much and do not throw any challenge to the other party. This is a very poor option compared to option 2. When you go for option 2, you are making the negotiation worth the while for the other party. In option 2, the other party may end up paying more than they would for option 1, yet they would be far more satisfied with themselves, because they met with some challenge. Although this is counterintuitive to economic logic, research has proved that the level of satisfaction of any negotiator is high when they have had to work their way towards a good final price vis-à-vis closing at a price straight away.

Option 3 is a lame one. You may intend to be fair and to develop trust, but this can work against you. The other party sees greater value in what you are offering, but you don't; well, perhaps the quality offered is substandard? This strategy has a good chance to backfire.

Conclusion

Spell out your WAP in absolutely clear terms before entering a negotiation. At the same time, determine for yourself the things you are okay compromising on. Once you are at the negotiation table, be the first to make an offer (hoping you have worked on your BATNA and anticipated theirs).

Chapter challenge: The unreasonable offer

Find something at home of less value that you are willing to part with, preferably something new and not so common. A uniquely designed mug, a fancy pen, a smart keychain are a few examples that come to the top of my head. Next, find an appropriate time and place to offer it to someone you know. Tell them you have something very interesting to sell that they could use for various purposes and would immensely benefit from. Having grabbed their attention, make your opening offer and keep it on the higher side. You have intentionally placed an anchor on them, so enjoy noticing how your opening offer steers the entire negotiation. Once you've made your point, you may end the negotiation and share your experiment with them.

Chapter 5

Eye for the Irrefutable Five

Secrets to Achieving What You Deserve

Regardless of the volume, weight or height of the negotiation, there are five aspects that cannot be overlooked. No negotiation can be effective unless all of these are considered before, during and as a reflection after every negotiation.

The irrefutable five are:

Parties	Negotiate with those that have the power, the authority and the desire to buy or sell
Value	Know what the other party values and deliver on that
Barriers	Recognize the dead ends, accept them and move on

Power	Empower yourself to gain solid advantage in negotiations
Ethics	Be aware that nothing is worth gaining at the cost of ethical values

Parties

We must know whom we are negotiating with. The car salesperson has clear instructions in terms of the max they can offer. The guy you need to negotiate with is the manager of the showroom, not the salesperson. When you are selling a home, you need to have some really interesting things to show and tell to the woman and children of the man. After all, they are the ones to finally call the shots in terms of where they are going to live.

Getting the right people in the room to negotiate with is critical. I remember my X company's HR head interviewing the incoming CEO, i.e. his potential boss. You can imagine how the salary negotiations went; the HR head felt obliged to reveal the highest possible salary and gave it to him. He had no choice because the moment the CEO walked into the office, he would have full access to everything!

We must understand who has the ultimate authority to finalize or close the deal. So much time is wasted when we are negotiating with paper pushers. Get the right people and the probability of getting what you want is quadrupled.

How do I know I am speaking to the right person?

One way to assess if you have the right people across the table to negotiate with is ensuring they have the **money** to afford what you are offering, the **authority** to take decisions and the **desire** to own your product or use your service. The HR executive wants to engage an external vendor (has desire) but cannot finalize without their manager's approval. It would hence be prudent to have them both when looking for a major or quick decision. Authority would include those who take final decisions or those who have a strong influence on those that take decisions.

Power to discern

We need to exercise caution when we discern who the right party is. While it's important to size up the other party to ensure we are negotiating with the right person, we must be cautious while making that assessment. In 1920, Jai Singh Prabhakar, the Maharaja of Alwar, bought seven new Rolls-Royce cars and employed them for garbage collection after he was refused a test drive in England. He was casually dressed when he visited a Rolls-Royce showroom in England where his request for a test drive was refused. After the Maharaja's unexpected move, Rolls-Royce apologized to him in writing because the Maharaja's move damaged the credibility of Rolls-Royce a great deal.

Value

If someone is thirsty and I offer them thirty-six varieties of food, they would simply reject the food, regardless of how tasty or sumptuous it might be.

In every negotiation, both parties vie to maximize their value. Understanding the other party and knowing what value they are trying to gain will then help me think in those terms while trying to make them understand how helping me would help them. I first understand you without any filters, and then I have you understand me. While we may not always be able to achieve a win-win, our intention as we begin any negotiation will determine the direction of the deal. We may land up win-lose or lose-win, nevertheless great negotiators look to seeing how they can enhance value for both parties.

In the business context, I remember working with a Royal Kuwati businessman who owned many quarries in Fujairah and was in the process of constructing residential mansions on a man-made island. He would love to do business with me for two simple things: reliability and speed. I was his go-to guy for any support that he wanted for his projects. If I did not understand clearly what **value** he sought and thought that I must simply offer him an attractive price or a flexible service, I would have lost that long-term client. When I understand truly what the other party values and deliver on that, then I stand a far better chance of getting my goals and objectives fulfilled.

When we look at negotiations in our personal relationships, money is usually not the greatest value we seek. Active listening, deep understanding, empathy and sincere appreciation top the value list. When we make the effort to know what value the other person seeks and we are able to deliver that to them, negotiations become a breeze.

American author Napoleon Hill specifies motives that people seek. When trying to convince anyone, if we can address their motive, we have a deal. Following are six such motives he mentions:

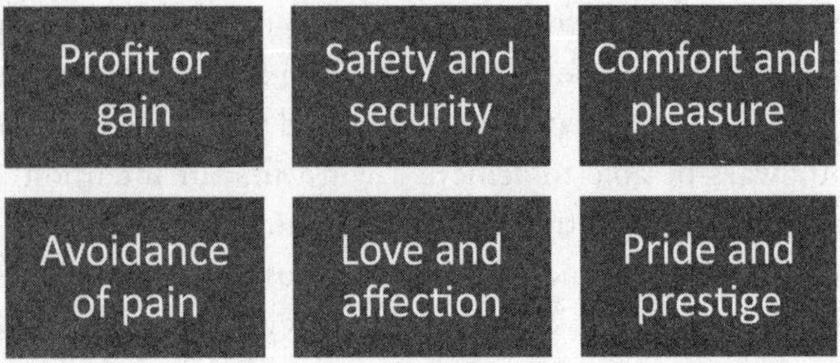

Negotiators must understand that people have developed a deep sense of fear after the pandemic. Hence, the value they are seeking is safety and security. As leaders, we must be able to assure safety and security to our people and customers before we expect them to be invested in us.

This aspect of knowing value and delivering value gets a negotiator up to a whole new level of success.

Barriers

On how many occasions have you approached people to get something done, but they have simply refused, directly or indirectly, leaving you exasperated and frustrated each time you tried? You go to the extent of giving up anything they demand, but they simply don't budge. Eventually, you realize you have wasted your time and energy and should have let go much earlier.

Whilst we endeavour to negotiate well, there are some barriers that restrict and tie us down, rendering useless our capability to achieve excellence.

In my previous company, we had a long-standing contract with a renowned multinational company. They wanted to make a change in our contract that would have virtually no commercial impact but would expect us to change a long-standing policy. I took the matter up with my chairman and he flatly refused to acknowledge stating that it was a subject that was not negotiable. He was okay with losing the client even. I went back to the client and requested that we find a workaround, but they refused, and consequently we lost one of our biggest accounts. I held myself guilty for long until my immediate boss called me and said, 'There are some very strong **institutional barriers** to negotiations; recognize them and accept them.' These barriers could be impregnable, so there is no point in wasting energy trying to negotiate.

Similar to institutional barriers are **psychological barriers**. People hold prejudices, stigmas, fears and beliefs that make it impossible to negotiate. I remember a client who signed a deal for a house, paid the down payment and was going to take possession. In came his 'Vastu' expert-friend, who found the house beautiful in every sense, but since it had a south-facing entrance, they refused to take possession. They forfeited the down payment but did not pursue the house any more. No amount of convincing, concessions or value adds made sense to them now. They would not take the house even if offered at 50 per cent its value.

Recognizing barriers

What are the signs of barriers you can recognize in the early stages so you can let go early?

1. Receive no response whatsoever: When the other person doesn't even acknowledge what you are saying or suggesting, understand that there is more in there

than meets the eye. Try different approaches but keep your hopes low.

2. Increasing list of complications: A client meant to pay a good sum to my colleague, but each time my colleague approached them, they kept asking him to come back with documents that were impossible to obtain under the circumstances he was in. Three years later, he gave up knowing they were trying to dodge him because he did not have strong evidence to claim his right.
3. Companies in doldrums: People can be buried in debt and so can organizations. While they may not openly admit it, you need to sense that as early as possible.

Power

You are powerful if you have within you the capacity to change the architecture of the negotiation. This can take place in many ways, and you may short-change yourself by assuming that just because you are the customer or the buyer, you are more powerful than the seller. Recently, I had put up a piece of land I wanted to sell. My broker introduced me to a prospective buyer who was very influential and seemed to be very powerful. I had a certain price stated and the buyer thought he could get his way to squeeze me into going down by 10 per cent on my quoted offer. I did not realize how powerful I was until I met him. I told him that I would love to have the deal closed with him, nevertheless, I am willing to wait until I get the price I seek. I was in no hurry to close. He listed out many things about the piece of land that made it unsuitable for any buyer and told me that it would not be an easy sell. But I was able to negotiate calmly and without a sense of desperation because I'd done my research about the market, had a strong BATNA and had determined a clear WAP for the deal. We parted as friends. In five days, he called back and said he was willing to pay me the quoted price. We closed the deal. This is when I realized how such subtle powers can make you a successful negotiator.

Ways to increase power

1. Communicate effectively: It will help you to speak and listen in a way that will get you the results you want.
2. Be competent at what you do: It will inspire confidence in the other party and shape their perception of you
3. Develop a character that is stable, reliable and ethical: It will help you navigate the responses of the other person with clarity.
4. Be emotionally strong: It will give you a huge advantage over those who lose their cool easily or get driven by their ego.
5. Show no desperation: Patience is a great virtue in negotiations as it pushes the other party to believe you have various options and do not care too much about the outcome.
6. Have a strong BATNA: It will give you the required confidence to negotiate your terms.
7. Be on time: It will give you an advantage to settle in, break the ice, get familiarized with the environment and add some quiet time before the negotiations begin.

Building power through a letter

A college student sends her parents a letter filled with disastrous news. I have reproduced the letter here, the origins of which are quite unclear:

Dear Mom and Dad

It has been three months since I left for college. I have been remiss in writing and I am very sorry for my thoughtlessness in not having written before. I will bring you up to date now, but before you read on, please sit down. You are not to read any further unless you are sitting down, okay.

Well then, I am getting along pretty well now. The skull fracture and the concussion I got when I jumped out of the window of my dormitory when it caught fire shortly after my arrival are pretty well healed by now. I only spent two weeks in the hospital and now I can see almost normally and only get those headaches once a day.

Fortunately, the fire in the dormitory and my jump were witnessed by an attendant at the gas station near the dorm, and he was the one who called the fire department and the ambulance. He also visited me at the hospital and since I had nowhere to live because of the burnt-out dormitory, he was kind enough to invite me to share his apartment with him. It's really a basement room, but it's kind of cute. He is a very fine boy and we have fallen deeply in love and are planning to get married. We haven't set the exact date yet, but it will be before my pregnancy begins to show.

Yes, Mom and Dad, I am pregnant. I know how very much you are looking forward to being grandparents and I know you will welcome the baby and give it the same love, devotion and tender care you gave me when I was a child. The reason for the delay in our marriage is that my boyfriend has some minor infection which prevents us from passing our premarital blood tests and I carelessly caught it from him. This will soon clear up with the penicillin injections I am now taking daily.

I know you will welcome him into the family with open arms. He is kind and although not well educated, he is ambitious. Although he is of a different race and religion than ours, I know that your oft-expressed tolerance will not permit you to be bothered by the fact that his skin colour is somewhat darker than ours. I am sure you will love him as I do. His family background is good too, for I am told his father is an important gunbearer in the village in Africa from which he comes.

Now that I have brought you up to date, I want to tell you there was no dormitory fire; I did not have a concussion or a skull fracture; I was not in the hospital; I am not pregnant; I am not engaged. I do not have syphillis, and there is no African in my life. However, I am getting a D in sociology and an F in science; and I wanted you to see these marks in proper perspective.

Your loving daughter

This letter is a classic case of how the daughter transfers power towards herself. Should she have spoken about her grades at the outset, she would seem weak and could be defensive, expecting the usual rebuke from her parents. However, once she was able to bring to light the possibilities of her behaviour, and made them believe in it, and then by negating it completely, she transferred full power to herself. And eventually, when she revealed what she wanted to, she was by no means in a weak position. In fact, she made the situation look so trivial compared to the rest of the behaviours that it would have come as a relief to her parents.

Power plays a very important role in negotiations.

Ethics

Negotiation is not simply about getting something you want at the moment. What you do and how you do it remain etched in you through your life. Therefore, it's important to be clear about your principles so you come out clear in your conscience. I have outright refused to do business in a few countries as I knew that getting businesses from them would mean bribing the employees of the large companies there. If I am approached to train them, where the deal is clean, I readily accept. I don't encourage bribery, and to me, the best way to discourage it is to not allow my greed to get the better of me.

Many of my colleagues take their clients out for drinks and that seems like a nice way to get what they want. I have never done that in my entire career because I don't drink and I will not do that for the sake of growing my business. Fulfilling this principle for me is much more important than closing deals.

I had organized an evening of fun and dine for my clients and their families where I ensured we had games arranged as well as competitions, music, dance and live entertainment and yet we did not serve alcoholic beverages. Initially, there were plenty of raised eyebrows. The following day, I received wonderful feedback for having organized such a wonderful evening sans the drinks. My clients and their families found the concept unique, creative and refreshing. My clients had fun and so did their families.

There are many companies that are highly ethical, whether it is in terms of accepting bribes, the way they treat their employees or the kind of businesses they are ready to enter. There are clear ethics and values they do not violate.

Azim Premji is a business tycoon, an ethical giant, a magnanimous philanthropist and an inspirational corporate leader with a net worth of over $7.2 billion. His company, Wipro, boasts ethical standards second to none. They refuse to give or take bribes from anyone. As a result, their factory had to be closed down for over twelve days at one point, suffering major disruptions, but they chose to take the hit rather than compromise on their ethics.

Conclusion

Amplify your negotiations whenever you can. Increase your awareness in the areas of parties, values, barriers, power and ethics. Run your radar around these irrefutable five prior to any negotiation.

Chapter challenge: Connecting the dots

Think back to a recent negotiation and run the details through the following worksheet:

1.	Did you have the right parties across the table to negotiate with?	Yes/ No	Who else could have been considered as important in the negotiation?	
2.	Did you dig deep enough to uncover the real value that the other party was seeking?	Yes/ No	What values, aspirations and fears did you uncover?	
3.	Were there any barriers that made the negotiation difficult?	Yes/ No	What were those barriers?	
4.	Were the power dynamics distinct in the negotiation?	Yes/ No	What did you do? What could be done to tilt the power dynamics in your favour?	
5.	Did you consider the ethical aspects in the negotiation?	Yes/ No	What ethics did you hold that were non-negotiable?	

Having filled out the above chart, ask yourself, 'What were some of the valuable lessons I learned and what will I do differently in future negotiations?'

Chapter 6

Principled Negotiator

Unleashing Your Inner Dealmaker

A key objective of this book is to change the way negotiations are usually perceived, be it in terms of its ubiquity, possibilities or its nature. Negotiations are for everyone: they are vital for enriching our lives, in helping us achieve our goals and need not be tarnished as a stressful and negative process. This chapter on principled negotiations, based on the Harvard Negotiation Project, will skilfully highlight these aspects for us.

William Ury and Roger Fisher, authors of *Getting to Yes*, were members of the Harvard Negotiation Project. The book suggests a method of principled negotiations or 'negotiation of merits'. Its purpose is to reach agreements without jeopardizing business relations.

It is counterintuitive to the belief many have around negotiations, that you need to be shrewd, lie, cheat and mislead the other party.

This method is based on four principles:

1. Separate person from problem
2. Focus on interests, not positions
3. Generate possibilities
4. Use of standards

Separate person from problem

When we negotiate, we need to be mindful of two distinct yet easy-to-overlook aspects. One is the person and the other is the problem. While the person is who we negotiate with, the problem is what we are trying to resolve, and hence it is very important to distinguish between the two and tackle the problem on its merits. If we mix the two, the negotiation becomes an uphill task; when we separate them, things become far smoother.

It is good to consider the person as the messenger of the problem, i.e. they cannot be victimized for the problem. This notion makes me more open and available without any distractions of sorts. Imagine I am negotiating with someone to get her to stop using her mobile often and she is constantly refusing; I may just call her a 'stubborn' person and give up. But if I do not mix the two, I try to understand the person's problem in a better way and then find alternatives or suggest better ways. In this case, the problem could be that the person is unable to disconnect from work even after office hours. I help them address the problem by sharing some techniques for mindfulness and better work–life balance.

When we don't do this, we end up being very hard on the person, and then when we upset them, we easily give in due to guilt. The logic in negotiation is that **the harder you want to be on the subject/substance, the softer you need to be on the person**—the skills of a diplomat, in other words.

Another point to ponder upon is that understanding someone and accepting their point of view is not the same as agreeing with them. We might disagree with them, but, it is important that they feel understood. Hence we agreeably disagree! This now becomes more palatable.

In a corporate setting, Anita, a sales manager, was approached by her sales executive Shyvon requesting that the latter get a few hours off every week. Shyvon was already enjoying a great amount of time off from work and it was quite a ridiculous proposal for her to put forth. During the conversation, Anita skilfully upheld this principle. She maintained the right perspective without becoming emotional about the demand and tackled the problem on its merits. She produced relevant data to prove that the executive was already getting benefits which the other colleagues were not enjoying. Besides, it was a very busy season, and hence it was not feasible for any further leeway at the moment. This way, Anita had a very positive conversation with Shyvon, and although Anita did not give in to the demands, she handled the situation with absolute poise and Shyvon returned satisfied with the outcome.

Very often, we have some fear lurking within us, and we project our fear on the intention of the other person. The other person, who may be an investment banker, could be speaking the absolute truth to us but because we have had a bad experience in the past with another investment banker, we refuse to believe what they are saying and doubt their intention. Even before they utter a single word, we discount everything by donning a mental block.

Considering the biases, beliefs and experiences we carry with us, separating the person from the problem may not be as easy as it seems, yet this is the first principle that underpins the success of any negotiation.

Focus on interests, not positions

Two men were having a squabble in a library. One demanded that the window be open and another for it to be closed. One claimed that he was a regular to the library, and this was a usual practice, while the other claimed that since two months this practice had stopped. They continued the argument when the librarian finally came to their rescue. 'Why do you want it open?' she asked the first guy. 'Because I want some fresh air in the library, it is quite stuffy.' 'And why do you want it closed?' she asked the other. 'To avoid the draft as it keeps making my papers fly away and I find it difficult to hold them.' 'Okay,' she said, 'I have a solution that will do both of you good.' She goes to the other end of the library and opens the window there. That way, there was plenty of fresh air without the draft disturbing anyone. Both were content and the librarian went back to her duty.

Often we make demands and claims and speak about terms and conditions without stating the underlying interests, motives, reasons or fears. Once we as negotiators dig deeper and move from positions to interests, we arrive at solutions; otherwise, we get into a stalemate where no one benefits.

There are many problems that we face on a daily basis that can be resolved through this principle. My teenage nephew would never want tomato in his sandwich and this was getting cumbersome for his mother. She kept demanding that he start eating them and that they are beneficial. He simply said, 'I don't like them,' and stopped at that. I inquired what it was that he really did not like about tomatoes, and he said, 'I don't like the seeds.' 'If the seeds were removed, would you be comfortable? I asked. 'Of course,' he said. There has never been a fuss about this since that day.

Let's go on to something bigger. Israel had captured most of the Sinai Peninsula from Egypt, a place that was exceptionally valuable to Egypt. Egypt claimed Sinai belonged to it, while Israel agreed but stated that now they occupied it, hence would not budge. They were stuck in this position for years. There were ongoing wars, but Egypt wasn't successful in regaining it. Eventually, they negotiated but moved beyond positions into interests and fears. Egypt opened up that while Sinai belonged to them, various invaders from the Gulf and beyond kept snatching it away from them. Eventually, they gained it back only to lose it to Israel. Sinai was sacred for Egypt and they wanted sovereignty over it. Israel said that if it gave Sinai back to them, it feared that Egypt would place all its artillery in Sinai, posing a constant threat to the people of Israel. So, a treaty was finally reached that lasts to date. Israel would give Sinai back if Egypt promised to not have any military presence in Sinai. They agreed. Egypt had its flag on Sinai with complete sovereignty while Israel had a peaceful border. There are such possibilities when we move away from positions and focus on interests.

Generate possibilities

When we enter a negotiation, we start off believing that there is perhaps only one way out or a few alternatives. However, once we truly understand the interests of the parties, then through creative and divergent thinking, we can collectively come up with surprisingly apt alternatives that are mutually beneficial.

When I was a sales executive providing waste solutions to corporates, we smashed our competitors by an innovative idea of building a dump site in town from where large-sized trailers would carry waste to the municipal dump yard thereby reducing our trip cost by one-third. Shortly, we went out to the market and slashed their trip cost by more than 50 per cent. Our competitors went berserk and did not know what to do. They immediately called for a meeting with an intention to make us change our strategy. Initially, we stuck to our guns and said we would continue with what we had done and did not trust that we could jointly do anything favourable. However, once we agreed to sit in the meeting and discuss possible options for the benefit of all, we were surprised at the outcomes. For the first time in the history of our industry, we started speaking about each other's interests and the various ways in which we could achieve mutual benefit. We decided not to poach each other's clients, standardized our rates, started sharing best practices, jointly represented municipal authorities for concessions and got discounted rates from our suppliers. Each and every one of us gained immensely from this and achieved unbelievable profits.

There is great synergy that we can generate through this principle.

While generating different possibilities, we need to bear the following in mind:

- Separate the creative process of inventing possibilities from the logical process of judging them: Inventing is a generative process. In the early stages of brainstorming for ideas, the emphasis should be on the free flow of creative ideas rather than on the practical aspects of execution.

- Broaden your options: I consider losing weight and I am in a negotiation with my spouse about the diet I must start having. If she does not comply fully with my demands, I would be better off if I had other options such as exercise, meditation, lifestyle shifts and so on. To be more successful at negotiations, it is important to broaden one's options rather than looking at things with a very narrow lens.
- Look for mutual gain: I want to lose weight and hence stick to a particular diet. My wife finds that inconvenient. She feels that I could cheat on two days of the week when we as a family can enjoy a restriction-free meal. Since I have many more options to support my goal, I cheat two days on my diet and make up with exercise and games. This way, we all get to win.
- Make decisions easy: The best way to do this is to listen to the other party and show them how the proposal will meet their goals. Once a relationship of trust is established and they clearly see how they will benefit from the proposal, making a decision becomes very easy.

Use of standards

I remember once going to my landlord and requesting that he reduced the rent by 10 per cent. The market was down at that time, and hence the request that he made a consideration.

I pitched the request at 10 per cent with a hope that I would at least get 5 per cent, but my request fell on deaf ears. I returned a week later. I provided the landlord with statistics that showed how many landlords in the vicinity had reduced their rents by 10–15 per cent. It was a standard practice whenever the markets were down. He was more convinced this time and reduced the rent by 7.5 percentage.

When we make a request for a change, it is good to support that request with a standard, a precedent, a market value or an industry practice. This way, we get better results. It is important to bear in mind that his standard or precedent is widely accepted and relevant.

Here are some of the standards we can use in different types of negotiations:

Salary negotiations	Competitors, percentage of growth in business, inflation, etc.
Selling products	Percentage increase in raw material cost, percentage increase in average cost, prevailing prices of similar products in the market, additional taxes/charges (and similar standards that are both relevant and accepted)
Buying products	Percentage decrease in raw material cost, percentage increase in volume/frequency, prevailing market prices, reduced taxes/charges (and similar standards that are both relevant and accepted)

Conclusion

By becoming a principled negotiator, you not only succeed in your day-to-day negotiations, you develop and build credibility among your contacts. Word spreads soon about you and, for future negotiations, your reputation will precede you!

Chapter challenge: The tough get going

Consider a potential negotiation with someone tough that you have always put away for another day. Think through the negotiation now in light of the four principles. Visualize the entire negotiation chronologically, beginning with 'separate person from problem' all the way to the 'use of standards'. Realize that if the principles are used well, there will be great outcomes. With that confidence, call for a meeting and be awesome.

Chapter 7

Trust and Responsibility

Navigating the Negotiator's Dilemma

The HR head of 'The Utility Company', Ras Al-Khaimah's power supply company, approached me to conduct a half-day leadership training for their business unit heads. These were my initial days of business as a full-fledged trainer. I was asked to do this session free of cost with a promise that if they received good feedback from the participants, then I would be their primary trainer for a host of training programmes that was in the pipeline that year.

This proposal put me in 'the negotiator's dilemma'. Cooperate and do the training free of cost or compete and ensure I get paid or am given concrete guarantees for my services. I decided to cooperate. We designed an astounding session and the feedback far exceeded our expectations. The HR head was highly impressed and confirmed that I would be the one to train the leadership team on a host of titles. I was so glad I cooperated, especially because I was certain that our delivery would be brilliant. Here's the twist: I followed up with this guy for four years after our training and he did not give me a single session. Why? Their chairman, who was not part of our training, decided to have a good friend of his train their leadership team and the HR head could not veto that. My lesson: I readily created value for the prospect, but I was clumsy in claiming value for myself.

While every negotiator tries to maximize their own earning, there are two distinct things that are expected of an able negotiator: **claim value** for the self and **create value** for the other party. In order to claim value for the self, we need to be **assertive** and in order to create value for the other party we need to be **empathetic**. So there is this constant tension between these two: how much to claim and how much to create, how much of assertion and how much of empathy. The chart below shows that if we do not strike a balance between being assertive and being empathetic, then we are either aggressive or docile and hence we claim too much or create too much.

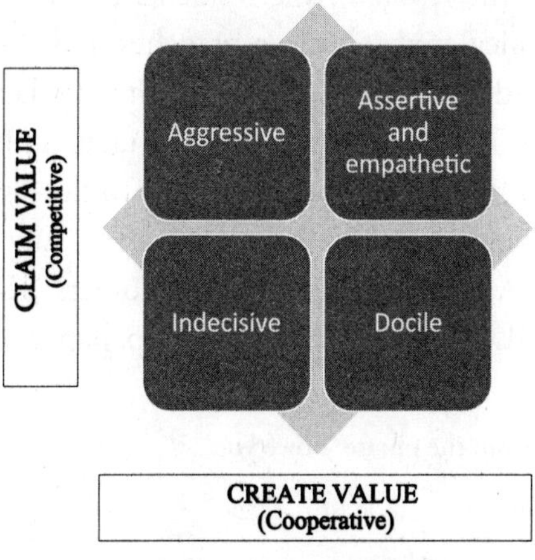

Being on the extreme side of the scale for too long would be disastrous. We could look at this delicate balance as similar to flying a kite. We need to pull the string while we let loose, and this tug of war must continue for the kite to fly.

Trust with responsibility

It is important to begin any negotiation positively. We want to really understand the other person, what their interests are, consider if they are acknowledging our cooperation and being cooperative too. Think win-win and seek first to understand. It is important to know that trust begets trust. Negotiation is a two-way street. I love to share a story on trust that may sound unbelievable, but it works.

In 2005, Hurricane Katrina took the US by surprise and largely affected the Mississippi. The banks in the region were closed and the ATMs weren't functioning. The residents had no way of withdrawing money from banks or ATMs and were thus rendered cashless. The employees of Hancock Bank stepped up and came to the rescue of the residents of Mississippi. They collected money from all their branches and ATMs (which were apparently dirty and drenched), literally laundered and pressed them. They then set up tarp and tables in front of their branches and started distributing money to the residents.

They paid $43,000,000 in cash. Advances were available to everyone, not just its customers. IDs were not required. IOUs[6] were written on scrap paper and Post-its.

[6] Abbreviated from the phrase 'I owe you'.

Five months later, all but $200,000 was repaid (99.5 per cent of the advances). Hancock got 3000 new accounts and its deposits increased by $1.5 billion.

Cooperation is a good opening strategy, and we must bear in mind that while it would work in a majority of occasions, there may be times when it backfires, as it did for me with The Utility Company. However, in that case, I blame myself for the clumsy way in which I negotiated, i.e. being very submissive. I should have made them pay the standard fee with an assurance that it would be returned in case the feedback was poor.

I learn so I can lead

I have a beautiful array of strategies to choose from while negotiating. I could cooperate all the time or compete all the time. I could change my strategy from being cooperative to competitive if I find my opponent is being competitive despite my being cooperative. I could be slow to trust (compete unless I am convinced that the other party is repeatedly cooperative) or slow to anger (cooperate unless I am convinced that the other party is repeatedly competitive). While I would initially opt to cooperate with the person I am negotiating with, I would be very keen to learn how the other party responds. I would flex my negotiation strategy accordingly. Should the other party be highly assertive and is only thinking of claiming value for the self, I would choose to be assertive so I don't concede too much, but if the other party is empathetic and is keen to create value for me, then I don't have to be very assertive and could be more empathetic while my interests are being met. So, the only way to know what I must do is to read the other party. There are three steps to doing this:

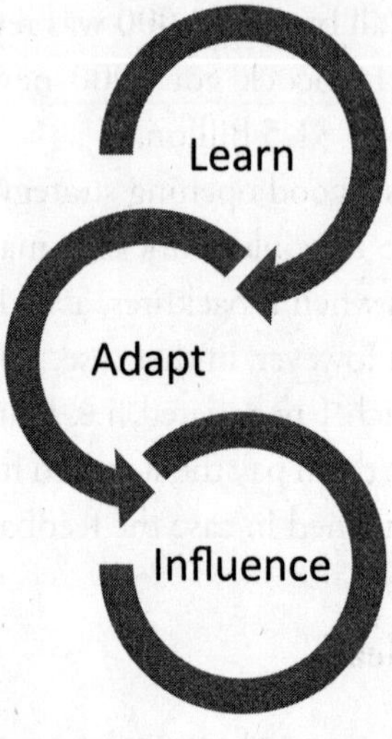

1. Learn: What is your counterpart's strategy and tendency? Are they sharks, wanting to take everything, every time? They like to have the last word and win every argument? Or do you see them conceding and letting you have a few things your way—listening to understand you before expecting to be understood? I have had clients who were more worried about the training fee than the content and outcome. They would be extremely pushy, they would not take no for an answer and would simply not listen. On the other hand, I have had clients who are genuinely concerned about the value they derive (return on investment) from the training workshops, have meaningful conversations around the content and are willing to shift their position based on logic and facts.

I have experienced two different planets! It is crucial for me to learn their behaviour as that would set the tone of the negotiation.

2. Adapt: Observe and orient to what unfolds. Your flexibility as a negotiator plays a vital role in how you steer the negotiation. On one hand, when you adapt, you match your style with that of the other party and then, when it is time, take the lead. This is where you develop a strong rapport, which is the starting place for developing relationships and bonds. On the other hand, when you see that your opponent is highly competitive and you are highly cooperative, you would land up being exploited. You need to adapt to the style that sends a signal to the other party that you know how to cooperate but will not allow yourself to be exploited.
3. Influence: As much as you can, try to make the other party cooperate so that they become empathetic to you. Offer rewards for their cooperation, and penalize them for being competitive. For instance, when my brother who owns a ready-made garment store charges a negligible amount to his customers who want their trousers altered, some of them understand and accept this without much fuss, and for them, he prioritizes and delivers within an hour. Some customers argue vehemently that this charge must be waived off and to them he says that they will get their trousers altered only after two days. The moment he says this, these customers quickly agree to pay for the alteration and begin requesting a faster delivery.

One of the most valuable lessons I took from the Learn, Adapt and Influence cycle is that it is very important for us to meet people where they are, and then walk them along in the direction that is beneficial to us. If you simply stand on one end, far away from the other person, and expect that they get over to your side, you may be asking for way too much, or it would be a very difficult proposition. Even as leaders in organizations, the only way we can exercise influence over others is by understanding our people, where they are, what their values are, what their culture is and what their aspirations are. **If you don't take the trouble to understand me, there is no way I can trust you to take me where I want to go.**

It is due to the importance of this that negotiation is often defined as learning, adapting and influencing in a strategic environment.

Shift from compete to cooperate

Here are four simple things that one can do to get the other party to be more cooperative:

Whenever I find the other party cooperating	Reward cooperation	This will anchor their behaviour and they will repeat it
When I find the other party repeatedly compete	Penalize the competition	They will realize that I am powerful and put them in the defense position

When I find the other party repeatedly compete	Withhold reward	Gives them a feeling of losing out on something of value
When I find the other party repeatedly compete	Become competitive	Shows that I am willing to lose if push comes to shove

Beware of Boulwarism

Lemuel Boulware was the vice president at General Electric. He was very aggressive in the way he bargained and adopted a policy of take-it-or-leave-it. He primarily used it with vendors to GE. They would all be invited into a meeting and simply asked to drop their contract value by 10 per cent if they wanted to continue working with GE. If they could not do so, then they may simply take their business elsewhere. His policy became so prominent that today this technique in negotiation parlance is known as Boulwarism. Someone engaging in Boulwarism is extremely aggressive and brings absolutely no empathy to the table. They want it their way, always claiming value and that is all about it. Boulwarism may instil resentment and bitterness or lead to someone taking offense. It may force the other party to cut corners or compromise on quality. It may unintentionally cut off negotiations if the offeror was bluffing about the offer being their bottom line, or the tactic may result in parties walking away from the negotiation.

Conclusion

Never get intimidated by anyone's negotiation style. Be courageous and curious. Learn their tendencies, match them and try to move them over to being more cooperative. This way, you maximize your returns and do not leave any chance for the other party to exploit you.

Chapter challenge: Guess who?

Be a champion of reading personalities. For the next few days, observe everyone you come across with respect to their orientation. Place them on a scale from being competitive to the core to being highly accommodative, with a learner's mindset. Look out for vendors, salespersons, business owners, executives and even people at home. What are the telltale signs of these personalities? What are their behaviours? How do they communicate? This exercise will hone your skill of learning what is happening on the other side, which is the starting point of choosing your strategy.

Chapter 8

Tackling Deception

Understand How Rules Get Broken

It is not uncommon to experience deception in negotiation; inflated numbers, concealed information, empty promises and ambiguous statements. Astute negotiators are required to detect these behaviours, although most can be very poor at it.

Let's look at a few examples. I am planning to buy a house in Dubai Marina, and the agent shows me around and invites me to the balcony from where I have a look at the exuberance of the sea right outside. I am very pleased and this is perhaps the only reason why I want to buy this flat. What the agent does not tell me, which she knows, is that in the next six months, another building would be right outside, covering the entire view of the sea. Or it could be a car dealer who talks to me about everything great and withholds information about the AC, which is usually weak in such cars.

What I have personally noticed is that in negotiations, mostly, the parties don't blatantly lie, but they find ways of being deceptive, i.e. they don't tell the truth as it should be told. Hence, when I enter any negotiation, I need to safeguard myself against such deception.

Listen keenly, ask directly and observe carefully

1. Listen keenly: It is important to listen to the words spoken including the body language of the person speaking. Watch out for shifty eyes, hand touching the face, swallowing or any display of discomfort. These signals should not be overlooked.
2. Ask directly: It is important that we ask direct questions with the intention to receive direct answers: Would you know if another building is proposed to come up here? I have read poor reviews about the AC of this car. Is it true that the car has a poor AC compared to the other brands?
3. Observe carefully for non-responses: When you ask direct questions, a deceptive person would weave their way around them in an evasive manner. They may speak about the building, such as 'Well . . . getting permissions to build is not easy here.' About the AC of the car: 'These ACs are built by Zenith, one of the top brands in the world.' If you observe carefully, you will notice that they are neither agreeing nor denying, but deflecting your question deceptively. So a good negotiator would ask questions and observe carefully for non-response. When you observe a non-response, it is

important to solicit clarity: 'So I will take it that there is a possibility of a building coming up in case permission is granted,' or 'Although the brand is Zenith, I take it that the review about the A/C is right.' In this way, you are showing that you are not one to be easily deceived by the words of the other party. Making such pointed rebuttals will reveal the truth and corner the other party.

4. Propose a contingency: There is a possibility that despite the non-response being caught and a pointed question posed, the other party blatently lies to us: 'No building will come up here anytime,' or 'This AC is superior to any other car manufactured.' In this case, it is best to propose a contingency: 'Okay, I will be happy to sign up and purchase this house from you, with a contingency in the contract that should any other building come up in the next five years, you are willing to hive 15 per cent from your initial offer,' or 'Should the AC perform poorly, you are willing to replace it.' When you make an offer to seriously include the clause in the contract, if they are being honest, they will be more than happy to do so or they would come out in the bare and state the truth.
5. Be well informed: Do your homework before you buy something. For example, when I was planning to buy a rowing machine, I went online, read a lot of reviews on that model and came to know that a pulley on this particular machine was likely to fail after a year's use. Hence, I was successful in getting a guarantee from them that they would replace the part if it failed within two years.

DETECT AND DEAL WITH DECEPTION

Deception telltales

There are many other ways in which we can sense that something is raw in the deal. The earlier you sense this, the safer you are:

- You are being rushed to make a decision: I have, many times, been trapped with this 'time pressure' tactic. This offer is valid only until midnight. You must decide immediately. Take it or leave it. Their pressure tactics need to be cautiously dealt with. The other party feels that if you are going to speak to others, and perhaps even to competition, then the truth would be revealed. Thus let's do it now, right here. I would like to take some time before deciding, especially where important matters are in question. Hence it is good to sleep over the offer, speak to some trusted people and only then move ahead.
- When the offer is too good to be true: When I have the other party start off with a very high offer and then goes down by 75 per cent in the next ten minutes or so, then I know that something is fishy. I need to be watchful and try to buy some

time before finalizing. I know of people who have negotiated in haste and committed to something just because the offer was unbelievably good and then found some major problem. Their entire investment goes down the drain.

- Get-rich-soon schemes/scams: Every tactic will be displayed before you. You will be shown documents, statistics and testimonials and made to believe that without their services/products, you are worthless. That is how I was made to feel many times by multi-level marketing executives.

Precautions in the face of foul play

Ever noticed how despite our hunch that there is something fishy in the making, we still go ahead and finalize the deal, only to regret it later? What precautions must we take when we suspect foul play?

- Do your due diligence: When we were hiring for the position of customer service executive, we finalized on a candidate who met all our criteria for the job. When he was speaking about his last work experience, we noticed that he was giving us shallow answers. That suspicion made us pick up the phone and speak to the HR in that company and we realized that this candidate did not work there at all, but his dad was employed there. Doing due diligence could be just a call away and we must exercise that without hesitation.
- Employ your six honest serving men: Ask questions that have to do with who, what, why, which, when

and how—Kipling terms them as 'our six honest serving men'. It is very difficult for deceptors to have all the bases covered. Hence, when we ask them this full range of questions, much gets revealed. The point here is to ask for the full range without missing a single one.

- Trust but verify: We may get trapped with people who are close to us, and we feel embarrassed asking them questions because we do not want to hurt them. It is critical to clarify at the very outset with such close contacts that you have a certain protocol before making any decision and you will be exercising the same even though there is absolute trust in the relationship. Get their explicit permission and specify all the questions that you seek clarity on. It would also make sense to have someone neutral get involved in case you have inhibitions about asking some questions. This way, you have a good check and not just get into certain agreements blindly.
- Use appropriate systems: A part of overcoming deception is to have accuracy of data and to ensure it is up to date. In businesses that have partners, all transactions must be transparent, well recorded, updated and accurate. Deception, for example, may seep in if the partners claimed expenses that took place months ago. I had a few colleagues who lived together in a bachelor's accommodation. They would delay settling their monthly bills on time and that created much confusion and speculation. When they were introduced to Splitwise (an app designed

to help people split costs in real time), they simply had to enter their bills into the system as soon as the expense occurred and they could check what was due from each member on any day of the month. This assured everyone of accuracy and helped maintain a healthy relationship among them. The notion of deception that may have existed due to human error got completely taken care of.

- Take swift action: Be swift in reverting to the party when you sense any deception. The longer one takes to get back, the more difficult it becomes to negotiate. The other party uses time to their advantage, and they try to get commitment at the earliest. Even if a commitment is made, the idea is to move quickly and convey your change in thought when you notice discrepancy, even if it is just a doubt. I have got into investments that I have pulled out of when I noticed something incorrect in the deal. The other party reveals that if I pull out, I lose whatever I invested, but that is fine; I do not want to waste good money trying to save money that is already bad. Stop the bleeding as soon as you can.
- Be a stickler for discipline: If you are disciplined enough to have things well accounted and shared, then it saves a lot of hassle later. It is important that you get the other party also to be disciplined through the deal. I had a bitter experience with a telecommunication company in the UAE. I had not requested for any entertainment service, but they included that automatically when they upgraded

my network. Each month I was being charged AED45 and I was not disciplined enough to check the monthly bills. Months became years and by the time I discovered it, I had already paid them an extra AED1200 for a service that I never used. When I asked them, eventually, they told me that although I did not request for the service, I was obliged to call them and cancel it and they would not refund the amount.

- Seek flexi-payment options: You are always in control if you haven't paid in full at the start. Stagger payments so you can always wriggle out of a deal that you find raw at any time.
- Do not judge a book by its cover: Negotiation demands that we go beyond people's looks and words. Caveat emptor. Looks and words could be deceptive. Hence, as naïve and innocuous the other party may seem, keep your guard up.

Conclusion

Be aware and astute when negotiating, in the anticipation of deception. This will keep you well poised to stay confident and to generate trust with the other party.

Chapter challenge: Mirror mirror on the wall

It is impossible to find someone who has not been a victim of deception. The greatest negotiators today have had the bitterest of experiences, yet they learnt from those experiences and moved on. Similarly, look back at your experiences when you have been a victim of deception and rather than feeling guilty or giving negotiations a bad name, reflect on the learning and step up. Here are a few reflective points to support you in this endeavour:

1. As I look back at a recent negotiation, what did I see, feel or hear which I overlooked but am aware of now?
2. What are some questions I could have asked?
3. What actions could I have taken to avoid being deceived?
4. What has been the greatest learning for me that I will bear in mind the next time I negotiate?

Chapter 9

Emotional Intelligence in Negotiations

Managing Feelings for Success

People have strong feelings about negotiation. The sale of a $3-million townhouse made news when the deal almost fell apart because of a washing machine. The buyer and seller had many rounds of discussions and when they were at the premises ready to sign off and receive the payment, the buyer requested that the washing machine in the house be replaced. The seller refused since they had already made many concessions. This upset the buyer, who ripped the seven-figure cheque in front of the seller and stormed out of the house. The seller regretted it and agreed to reduce the price by $300. Hours later, the buyer was found in a bar tending to his wounds where the broker convinced him to take the deal.

The impact of poor emotions in negotiations not only has a financial impact but has been responsible for the loss of lives in various situations. In one incident, the United Nations Command decided to trim a poplar tree that was obstructing the view of a vital checkpoint in North Korea. The North Korean soldiers, while negotiating that the tree should not be trimmed, lost their cool and crushed the skulls of two US soldiers with the blunt end of their axe head. The incident went down in history as the Korean Axe Murder and had the potential of flaring up into a war between the US and North Korea.

There are numerous cases of losses, violence and wars that could have easily been curtailed if emotions were kept in check during negotiations.

The Magic Mix: 50 per cent emotions and 50 per cent economics

In my classroom sessions, I ask for two volunteers. I tell the first one that I would be willing to part with $100 provided he/she gets to share some portion of the money with the second volunteer. If the second person doesn't willingly accept what you offer, you dont don't get the $100. I then ask the second volunteer that if he/she were offered $20 and the first one kept $80, would he/she be okay. 'Remember, you have done nothing to deserve any amount; all you are going to do is accept the amount and move on,' I inform them. Every time I have done this, I have had the second person bluntly refusing, stating that it is unfair, and unless they get 50-50 or at least $40, they will not accept. It is quite shocking that they are willing to forgo the $20 or even $30, which doesn't make any economic sense. This is because our emotions take over and drive the decisions we make.

Most deals are 50 per cent emotions and 50 per cent economics. We cannot go into a negotiation believing all that matters is numbers. As long as I have a financially viable offer, the other party will accept, but we need to consider emotions too, as they play an equally important role.

Who is responsible for the way I feel?

How would you like to feel before you enter any negotiation? Unanimously, if there is one word I have heard from experts and practitioners, it has been: we wish to feel 'positive'. The next question immediately sends them into a brilliant spin: who is responsible for making you feel this way? Instant response: 'myself', but after a few moments of contemplation, consideration and practical insights, they begin putting conditions such as 'depends on the other person', 'depends on the subject' and so on. I strongly feel that while most realize they are responsible for their feelings, mood and attitude, they somehow try to shrug off that responsibility, perhaps because they wish to be absolved of the guilt of losing themselves when negotiations get tense.

What the experts have to say

Herb Cohen, Chris Voss and a host of renowned international negotiators vouch for the fact that taking ownership of your state of mind and the ability to stay positive in negotiations are the greatest assets of an effective negotiator.

Care but not that much

According to Cohen, the way to stay positive in negotiations is to care for the outcomes of the negotiation but not care that much. Don't be too attached to the outcome, he suggests, only then will you be able to gain perspective and altitude, which, in turn, shapes your attitude. He suggests that we look at negotiations as a game, where we care but not *that* much.

Gain 30 per cent extra access to your brain

Voss draws from research that negotiators who are positive are able to access an additional 30 per cent of their brains versus those who are negative or disturbed by some negative emotion. Hence, his philosophy is simply to stay in an absolutely positive state while negotiating.

Emotions that blow negotiations away

Every emotion has the potential to damage a negotiation in one way or another. Listed here are the various emotions we may experience and their specific consequences.

The Emotion	Its Damage
Anger	Stalls negotiations and breaks relationships, sometimes permanently
Fear	Makes one over-compromise and give up too quickly
Anxiety	Causes one to be indecisive and reveals desperation
Stress	Leads one to make inaccurate decisions
Ego	Causes one to lose connection and communication with the other party easily

Power of pause

We are constantly subject to various moves, offers, suggestions or ideas from the other party. They come with a set of behaviours that could stimulate us to react in a certain way.

How do we manage our emotions so that we don't allow them to spiral out of control? One of the most powerful ways is through a 'pause'. A simple yet profound pause has the potential to diffuse any negative and unwarranted emotion.

In his book *The 7 Habits of Highly Effective People*, Stephen R. Covey provides us with a formula: Stimulus—Pause—Response. Usually we react immediately to a stimulus. We often get carried away and react to a negotiation with a negative emotion, so much so that we simply walk out with no deal at all or give everything away to the other side.

But if we are able to 'pause' and stay objective, we maintain our rational mind and can respond appropriately instead of succumbing to the stimulus. Hence, when we learn to effectively pause after a stimulus, we stay sane. An emotion is sometimes termed as **temporary insanity**, and we cannot afford to get into that state in the midst of a negotiation.

How long do you take a pause for?

The pause is not necessarily a function of time, i.e the pause is a psychological space I create where I understand well that I am fully responsible to create a response. The person, on the other hand, may offer whatever he/she wants, but I can instantly push the load aside, separate the message from the messenger and continue to have a sane conversation.

This demands practice and does not set in just by theoretically knowing that we have the capacity to choose our responses. While that is a start, we must become more reflective about our thoughts over time and start taking charge of our mind.

SOS (Stand back, Observe and Steer)

I practise SOS daily. I stop action, observe my thoughts and then steer them in a direction that is positive and productive. I do this regularly throughout the day, thereby mastering the art of managing my mind and setting it in a direction of my choice, and not allowing it to be driven by outside stimulus.

I am eliciting a visualization that I usually practise and that helps me expand awareness and sets me up for an empowered SOS. While reading the below visualization, slow down and make it real by picturing scenes as they are spelt out.

Visualize yourself standing on a railway platform, with trains arriving and departing from either side. You are simply observing the trains come and go; you are trying not to analyse what's happening around or control the trains but are simply available as an onlooker. Now, turn your thoughts inwards and look at yourself as the person standing on the platform of your mind, observing thoughts come and go but you do nothing to them—no analysis, no judgement, no controlling whatsoever. As an onlooker, you watch your thoughts flow.

The above exercise helps you with the first two parts of the equation, i.e. standing back and observing. Once you have done this effectively, you are ready to take up what you wish to focus on and steer your thoughts and actions in that direction.

Self-awareness rituals to work on our emotions

Working on managing our emotions is not a quick fix and must not be treated that way either. It is important to understand that it takes time to change old habits and if we have developed some bad habits that 'evoke' unwanted emotions when least expected, then we must build rituals that help us overcome them over time.

One of the greatest ways of tackling emotions is through heightened self-awareness. Additionally, through heightened self-awareness we can anticipate and navigate unexpected emotions from the other party, thereby staying in control of the negotiation process.

Here are some ways in which we can increase our self-awareness:

- Uncovering my values: The discovery of core values is the first step towards enhancing our awareness. Reflect on times when you have stood up for something, gone out of your way to be someone or done something that was important to the self or others, overcome challenges that came your way—in all these areas you definitely have exercised your core values. Uncover them and identify them. The next step is to accept them unequivocally. I am that value and that value is me, period. I may behave differently during the normal course of life, but that does not necessarily define my true nature. When I begin to come to terms and fully accept my values, I can start growing their presence in my life through journalling and mindfulness exercises, finding ways to positively channel them in my negotiations.

Through mindfulness, I bring myself to the present and become fully aware of everything I see, hear and feel, without judging or analysing anything. I then bring up one value at a time in my mind (confidence, for example). I contemplate on the meaning of this value and fully accept it by stating, 'I am confident and resourceful,' as I allow the words to sink in and make complete sense to me. I visualize myself embodying and demonstrating this value in my thoughts, words, actions and interactions with others. I experience the power and impact of this value. I then continue this exercise with different values and slowly but surely, over time, these values begin to grow within me and translate to my everyday interactions with people.

- Knowing my purpose: This is perhaps the greatest discovery of any human because once this is clear, everything else in my life becomes clear. I am able to make accurate decisions, execute them with absolute passion and overcome every obstacle or distraction that comes in the way of my journey. One way to discover your purpose is to look at yourself ten or twenty years hence and consider what you would like to be known for, what legacy do you wish to leave and what would you like others to say about you. Another way to do this is to look at nature and understand the reason for its existence, and then match that with our own. Our purpose, we would discover, usually pushes us to express our uniqueness in a way that helps and supports others unconditionally. Someone who is aware and consciously living their purpose looks at their negative emotions as obstacles and are able to free themselves of them over time.

- Practising meditation: 'Thoughts become things' is a popular saying. Meditation is an art and science that helps me focus on my thoughts and understand the root from where they emerge. It also guides me as I navigate my thoughts in a powerful and positive direction. When someone is practising meditation in the right way, over a period of time, they begin to have full control of their mind and choose their thoughts appropriately.

Conclusion

It is easy to ignore the intangible element of emotions in any negotiation. We could go in with utter confidence because we are well prepared and believe we have a powerful position. Be cautious because emotions always catch you when you are unaware of them. By simply becoming aware of the havoc they can create and by constantly checking and clearing them as soon as you sense them, you will be on top of your negotiation game.

Chapter challenge: Intentional inquiry

Begin journalling every night. Reflect and contemplate on your values, elaborate on them to deepen your relationship and connection with them, to the extent of embodying them in every possible way. Here are a few questions that will help you get started:

- What are some of the things I did today that make me feel good/proud? What values did I practise? How can I do this more often?
- What are some of the things I did today that were not very approving? What values did I compromise on? What have I learnt and what will I change?
- What can I do to remind myself of my values and experience them through the day?

Chapter 10

The Language of Negotiation

Verbal and Non-Verbal Mastery

A classic study was done in 1978 by Ellen Langer of Harvard University.[7] Three types of actors were asked to break a queue waiting to get photocopies done.

First set of actors were to ask:

- Excuse me, I have five pages. May I use the xerox machine?

The second set of actors asked:

- Excuse me, I have five pages. May I use the xerox machine because I have to make copies?

[7] E.J. Langer, A. Blank and B. Chanowitz, 'The mindlessness of ostensibly thoughtful action: The role of "placebic" information in interpersonal interaction', *Journal of Personality and Social Psychology*, 36(6), 1987, pp. 635–42.

The third set of actors asked:

- Excuse me, I have five pages. May I use the xerox machine because I'm in a rush?

The result? The first group got a 50 per cent success rate. The third got 93 per cent. The most surprising was the second group that got a 92 per cent success rate. Despite the fact that the second group showed no logic in explaining why they wanted to break the queue, they were allowed simply because they 'gave an explanation' by using the word 'because'. People did not bother so much about what the explanation exactly was before making a decision. Being asked a question with an accompanying explanation was good enough for them.

The words we use, the pauses, the silence, the active listening, our body language—everything plays a crucial role in our negotiations.

I look at communication not so much as just the exchange of ideas or only about speaking and listening. Simply put, communication is about **extracting the right response**. As long as I achieve what I want, I am effective in communication.

Persuading by using the 'rhetorical triangle'

I remember the time when I completed my MBA. I was already working as a sales consultant in a company for over three years. With my MBA, I felt I deserved a promotion. I knew I had to lay my cards right and so after a brief meeting where I conveyed my intention to my manager, I was asked to send him a formal letter. I thought through the contents of my message and decided to use the 'rhetorical triangle' model of persuasive communication, using 'ethos', 'pathos' and 'logos' to structure my proposition. I am breaking down the email that I had drafted here:

Dear Mr X

The last three years under your supervision have been one of my best years ever. Your guidance from the day that I walked into this company has been invaluable in my growth and development, and no words can justify the gratitude I hold deep in my heart.

(For the reader: I truly valued what I learnt from this boss of mine and could not but help open with a note of appreciation. I somehow felt that I had already received the promotion and hence had to say what I wanted to state for long. Once I did the edification with absolute sincerity, I was ready to step into building my credibility, i.e. ethos.)

Ethos (building my credibility): I feel so proud to be part of your team that delivered astounding results in the last two years and for bagging some of the most prestigious projects in the UAE. You trusted me with the hospitality sector and waste management of Sharjah and Ajman, and I cannot believe that these have grown to be our biggest revenue earners today.

Pathos (connecting emotionally): I have recently completed my MBA with a specialization in marketing. Considering the vision of growth of our company, I believe that I can add immense value in scaling our business and making you proud for the mentoring you have provided me so far. It has been three years since I have been in this department, and I have never approached you for a promotion but was waiting to prove myself and to be fully equipped before making such a proposal. I am sure you will see the aptness of this request.

Logos (use of logic): I have understood from the head office that a position for branch manager, East Coast, is vacant. I have read the job description and to my good luck, my profile fits the bill to a T. Through my MBA I have gained knowledge in the areas of strategy, finance, operations management and leadership; the branch manager's position will be perfectly apt in giving me an opportunity to put into practice such knowledge and wisdom gained.

I so look forward to your favourable response with eagerness.

Abundantly grateful,
Prakash Chugani

The outcome of the letter: one month later, I was given a promotion to head the regional office of the East Coast, which was unbelievably three levels higher than the position I was initially holding.

I am sure it was not all down to the letter, but there, the management did see potential in me before giving me such a huge responsibility; nevertheless, the letter was well structured and the contents reassured the leadership team to give me that role.

Raise your words, not your voice

The words we use make a huge impact on the other party. It is said that of unspoken words you are the master, of spoken words you are the slave. Hence, we must be careful of our choice of words. 'You look unprofessional' lands heavily, while 'Wearing this shirt makes you look unprofessional' sends the same message without being brash.

When using words, either orally or in writing, let us pay attention to the following five Cs:

1. Clear: The simplest way of defining clarity is 'saying what you mean and meaning what you say'. Another way to look at clarity is to ensure that the other party understands what you say as you intend.

   Our client once called us and asked us to supply them with five carpenters and we verbally agreed. When the personnel reached his location the following week, all were returned promptly. They actually wanted 'car painters' and not carpenters.
2. Concise: A well-known acronym in communication is KISS, i.e. Keep It Short Sweetie. Saying too much not only consumes time and energy but may also be counterproductive in negotiations. Say only what's needed. Brevity is indeed the soul of wit.
3. Complete: While keeping it concise, it is important not to swallow vital information. Say you tell a friend, 'We will meet at 2 p.m. at Mall of the Emirates.' There are several locations in the mall and besides, it would be better to specify the purpose of the meeting and for how long it will last.
4. Correct: The devil is always in the detail. The information we supply, in writing or in word, must be accurate in every sense. When I send an email stating, 'We will not tolerate any lose tyres,' I may not realize that I meant 'loose tyres'.

5. Considerate: There are some words that could be treated as rude or inconsiderate and we need to avoid them. I received a message from a colleague when I was in HR: 'I am glad to see your success in hiring this person for your department, but I only wish you gave equal importance to other departments.' I did not like it and would have appreciated that he speak to me personally rather than send me a message/mail to that effect.

Listening to the unsaid

No one can stop communicating. Even if they do not utter a single word, they are communicating through their body, their silence and their actions. Learning the finer aspects of non-verbal communication will help us go a long way in negotiations.

- Posture: Erect with shoulders open sends a signal of confidence and comfort to the other party.
- Eyes: They are the windows to a person's soul and reveal more than we realize. A genuine smile is visible through the eyes and not the lips.
- Face: Avoid touching the face while speaking or negotiating, otherwise you may give away signals of nervousness, confusion and even deceit.
- Hands: The hands have immense possibility to express and reveal many elements with accuracy and clarity. Here is a list of things that can be revealed through our hands:

Usage	Description	Visual	Example
Number	Show of fingers		Three strategies to be more effective communicators
Increase/ decrease	Adjusting the space between the index finger and thumb		We are forecasting big growth over the next quarter/ there is a little problem
Together or divided	Bring together and joining palms or pulling apart palms		I am certain that when we work as one team, we will find a solution
Being honest	Palms up and open		I have shared everything I know with you
Make a point	A vertical chop		There is no way this option will fail
Demonstrate confidence	Keep both hands together in a steeple position		Let me explain the benefits to you

- Proxemics: The distance we leave between people is termed as proxemics. The distance is much larger when interacting with strangers and may get smaller as the relationship is more intimate. Coming too close to a person you may not know very well could be very intimidating, hence this protocol must be addressed well.
- Handshake: A straight, firm and web-to-web handshake makes a good first impression, while a very soft 'dead fish' or a very hard 'bone crusher' sends an incorrect impression to the other party.
- Dressing: The way we dress and present ourselves speaks volumes about our seriousness about the meeting and our overall attitude. Research has shown that people who dress well are bound to get higher pay than those who don't, and the same applies with negotiations. There is one simple rule in dressing that would be of great value to anyone: dress like today is the most important day of your life. Two researchers at two different universities, the University of Illinois at Urbana-Champaign and UC-San Francisco, jointly published an article in the *Journal of Experimental Psychology* in 2014 **on the effects of formal attire on negotiations.**[8]

They invited 128 participants to play the role either of a seller or a buyer of a hypothetical company and randomly gave each an outfit to wear (formal or casual).

---

[8] Michael W. Kraus and Wendy Berry Mendes, 'Sartorial Symbols of Social Class Elicit Class-Consistent Behavioral and Physiological Responses: A Dyadic Approach', National Library of Medicine.

The purpose was to negotiate a price in six minutes. Here are the outcomes of the experiment:

- Participants who wore formal clothing obtained significantly higher profits
- Casually dressed men made more concessions than those in formal clothing
- When the person was negotiating with someone in formal clothes, he felt less powerful

Four communication hacks that will take you from good to great

1. Be precise in your pricing

Matthew Backus, Tom Blake and Steven Tadelis, all professors at Berkeley, carried out a research on whether we should quote whole numbers (rounded numbers or precise numbers).[9] They studied millions of offers made on eBay. They put possessions up with a fixed price and allowed others to bid against it. They found that round numbers had poorer results than precise numbers. Precise numbers suggest logic/reason. So the next time you want to make an offer for $10 million, think again. Set the price at $9,835,000.

---

[9] Matthew Backus, Tom Blake and Steven Tadelis, 'Cheap Talk, Round Numbers, and the Economics of Negotiation', National Bureau of Economic Research (NBER) Working Paper No. 21285, https://www.nber.org/system/files/working_papers/w21285/w21285.pdf

2. Don't be the one to say no

Daisy was being interviewed for a managerial position when she realized that the company was offering her almost 30 per cent less than what she was expecting. Besides, she was expecting some perks that were not part of the package. Once she heard what the company was going to offer, her first thought was to thank them and let them know that she wasn't interested before walking out of the deal. On second thoughts, she decided to let them know what she had been expecting. So, she put forth all her demands. While she felt she was trying to win a lost battle, she went ahead, laid her demands and requested that the company consider her proposal and revert. The next day, she received a call from the company stating that all her demands would be met. She was flabbergasted as she was at the verge of walking out of the deal. She thanked herself for not saying 'no' and for stating her demands and putting the ball in the other party's court.

3. Anchor the negotiation

As we discussed in Chapter 4, the first offer steers the negotiation. So, if you have enough information, be the first to make the opening offer. If you don't, allow the other to do so but avoid getting anchored to that offer especially if it is way out of the expected ballpark. See how you can quickly get the other person to know that you are aware of their unreasonable opening offer (in a light way) and bring them back on track. I had a girl in one of my negotiation sessions who said that when someone makes an unreasonable offer, she says, 'Wow! Thats an attractive price. If you know anyone making such an offer, let me know and I will buy their complete stock.'

4. Be an active listener

Nelson Mandela is considered one of the greats of all time. An exemplary leader, he had a very novel way of winning people over. When asked about the secret of his success, he said he had picked one trait from his father Gadla Henry that had proven exceptionally useful. Henry, who was a local chief, was called to chair many meetings. Young Nelson would accompany his father to some of these meetings. There, he noticed that his father was always the last to speak. Henry would first let others speak. He would listen to them with rapt attention and only when everyone else was done contributing to the discussion would he speak. Due to this rare trait, whenever it was his turn to speak, Henry would incorporate everyone's views and concerns, thus having the group's undivided attention.

Listening by itself is a good way of 'giving'. Giving others an opportunity to speak and be heard is a form of empathy which solicits the other person to give you this opportunity when you speak. Understanding begets understanding, hence listening is a fundamental requirement in any negotiation.

Zoom in while meeting virtually

With the increase in online negotiations, we cannot take for granted so many aspects that were hitherto in our control, be it the place of meeting, context, audiovisual clarity, freedom from interruptions and so on. Considering these, there are a few things to bear in mind that will support effective communication.

- Stay technologically prepared: Test your software and hardware well in advance. Log in a few minutes early as you cannot predict last-minute technical glitches.
- Be professional at all times: While you do have the opportunity to be casual in an online meeting, it is important that you impress the other party. Send them the meeting link well in advance, block their calendar, send a reminder an hour before the session and take notes during the session. Such actions keep you in good stead and add brownie points in your favour.
- Remain laser-focused: You do not have the luxury of seeing the entire body and all the gestures, so pay full attention to every detail that is displayed on your screen.
- Remove all disturbances: Noise can be a real distraction to you and the other party. Before getting knee-deep into the negotiations, clear all disturbances and request the same from the other party.
- Keep your respective videos on: You don't want to negotiate with a voice unless you have no better option.
- Get permission before recording: If you feel you need to record the session, ask permission explicitly.

Conclusion

You are communicating all the time and not just when you are speaking. The message that you are giving out, consciously and unconsciously, will steer the negotiation. By paying full attention to your verbal and non-verbal communication and by listening empathetically, you are much closer to getting the results you want.

Chapter challenge: Observe to measure

Watch a recording of a recent online meeting you have had. Observe your own tendencies of verbal and non-verbal communication. How do you compare with the other party and what are the implicit messages conveyed?

Chapter 11

Global Negotiations

Breaking Cultural Divides for Mutual Success

I was having a chat with my colleague who happened to work in Australia for many years and later settled in Dubai.

We began chatting about the importance of doing learning programmes online when I said, 'I feel it's a good idea to table the topic,' because I had other important stuff to complete and hence did not want to discuss this. 'Great idea,' she said and pulled out her laptop and started sharing the pros and cons of online learning. I was confused because I thought she agreed with me, only to later realize that it had to do with her Australian orientation.

In Australia, the phrase 'to table a topic' means to take that topic up and have a healthy discussion around it, while in the US, it means the exact opposite, where they are expected to stop talking about that topic. That opened up a very exciting angle to negotiations. When we are negotiating and communicating with different cultures, in addition to our skills in negotiations, we need additional skills: cross-cultural sensitivity.

Suspend all judgement

As we venture into this dynamic and nuanced subject of international negotiations, our endeavour is to support readers in understanding that we must orient ourselves with the culture of the people with whom we negotiate. While the concepts around negotiation may be universal, neglecting culture could be counterproductive to the negotiation process and may hamper positive outcomes.

Cultures vary from region to region, perhaps from street to street too. We will cluster groups based on some common elements that make their culture unique just so we can sensitize ourselves when we negotiate with them. This generalization does not make us oblivious of the fact that there will be many exceptions and does not intend to take away the individuality of the person.

We wish to steer clear of ethnocentrism and do not intend projecting one culture as superior to another, nor do we want to stereotype people from any culture. I hope this is kept at the back of our minds as we explore this chapter.

Not a word more, not a word less

To illustrate the need to recognize differences in communication, allow me to share a personal experience with you. I remember flying into New York from Dubai:

it was a direct flight, almost fourteen hours of flying, and from there I took a cab to a retreat centre in Catskill, around two and a half hours from JFK. After over sixteen hours of travel, I was sumptuously fed and then one of the volunteers, an American, Debra, asked me, 'So, Prakash, how are you doing?' 'I am doing very well, thank you.' 'Well,' she asked, what would you like to do now? Would you want to rest and catch up on some sleep, or are you ready for Karma Yoga, i.e. service in yoga?' I thought it was a pretty obvious fact that I wanted rest; still, I found myself saying, 'Well, I am okay to do Karma Yoga,' hoping Debra might recheck and ask me to rest awhile before getting into action. But she did just the opposite. She quickly ushered me to the vast garden of potted plants and asked me to water them. She demonstrated the first few, how, while I spray water on the plants, I do also invoke feelings of love and peace and share that with the plants. 'If you want any help, shout out for me. I will be in the library there.' Saying this, she went off.

While I enjoyed every bit of Karma Yoga, one big realization dawned upon me: when I speak to Americans, I'd better be as explicit as I can. I'd better say what I mean and mean what I say if I don't want to get into any kind of 'troublesome' or even 'awkward' situation. We have this well-known adage for the Americans: tell them what you are going to tell them, tell them and then tell them what you've told them.

Awareness of subtle differences in communication patterns has a tremendous impact on how we understand each other and achieve our results. Hence, culture plays a very important role in negotiations. Every country or region has its own nuances and if we do not take cognizance of that, we could have a raw deal, even if we are fantastic at negotiations in our own country, with our own people.

When you do business with the Chinese, they have a wonderful habit of suddenly creating long pauses before responding. That pause can be so overwhelming for some that they start thinking that the Chinese are upset and so land up giving extra concessions.

Talking about other countries, a big deal was almost closed between an American and an Arab from Saudi Arabia. The American was well versed in the principles of negotiation and did a fantastic job. He convinced the Arab, who confirmed that his company would appoint the American as their sole manufacturing consultant. The American, once all was confirmed, summarized the steps that he and the Arab were going to take. When the Arab heard the American do the summary, he was annoyed. *Does he not trust me?* he asked himself. *I have given him my word, so why is he repeating and reconfirming?* Guess what? The American lost that deal.

Contextually speaking

Americans and other Anglo-Saxon countries are **low-context cultures**, i.e. for them, signals, gestures and norms don't work as much as explicit words. On the other end of the spectrum you have countries such as India, China, Japan and the Arab world, which are **high-context cultures,** where you are expected to know/understand what is being said even if it is not said in those many words or explicitly stated.

It will help us understand why some cultures are high in context while some are low. A case in point is the game Pictionary. I remember playing it with my cousins for the first time. They were living together while I didn't. So when I was meant to have them guess the picture I was creating, I had to be very explicit in my drawing. Otherwise, they would not have come anywhere close to the answer. When it was a team of players that lived together, it was remarkably easier for them to guess 'ivory table' in five seconds by simply drawing a table with three legs, because they had an ivory table with three legs in their house. As far as I was concerned, the context was very low, but for my cousins who lived in the same house for a long time, the context was so high that they did not even have to be specific to convey a meaning.

Countries that have a long history and culture, especially those in the Middle East and Asia, have a very high context. Hence, things need not be specifically spelt out to them. I love a custom that the Arabs follow. All visitors are usually offered *qahwa* (Arabic black coffee) in a tiny china cup. The moment the cup is empty, it gets instantly refilled by the steward, and this process continues until the cup, when empty, is shaken by the hand and placed on the table. If the cup isn't shaken, it keeps getting refilled. When with the Arabs, these little norms of etiquette mean a great deal to them.

Erin Meyer has done considerable research on this subject. In her book *The Culture Map: Breaking through the Invisible Boundaries of Global Business*, she brings out the nuances of different cultures very skilfully.

Upgraders vs downgraders

The Russians, French, Germans and Dutch tend to be upgraders. When they speak, they usually use words such as 'totally', 'completely' and 'absolutely', although they do not literally mean that. I remember sending a document to a German client which had a schedule of full-day safety training that we had to impart to our outsourced staff. He got back to me on an email saying that he found the schedule unacceptable and was out of sync. When I called him, all he wanted me to change was that I allow for an hour break instead of forty-five minutes. I was expecting a huge debate over many other aspects of the schedule but later realized that I was dealing with an upgrader.

Those from Mexico, Thailand, Japan, Peruvia, the Middle East, India and Southeast Asia tend to be downgraders. They usually use words such as 'partially', 'a little bit' and 'maybe' but do not literally mean that. I once had an Indian boss who would ask me if I had a minute, and when I said yes, he would continue speaking with me. The conversation would usually run into hours.

If a Russian says, 'I completely disagree with you. This is totally absurd,' his counterparts know he is ready for a hot debate and is simply soliciting a spirited conversation. When an Arab hears this, he might believe that the problem is bigger than it really is.

Contained vs expressive

When it comes to emotions, Brazil, France, Mexico, Saudi, India and the Philippines are expressive, whereas Denmark, Germany, the Netherlands, the UK, Sweden and Korea are contained. So you would have the French behaving very emphatically, revealing more than necessary as to how he is feeling. You may think he is very pleased with your offer but don't be surprised if the deal is not closed with you. Whereas a German may be very pleased with your offer but would be highly contained emotionally. You may misread this thinking he is not happy with your offer and be tempted to sweeten it.

The Japanese and the Chinese find it very hard to say no to anyone directly. That is why you should not ask them, 'Can you deliver this in two weeks?' They would find it extremely difficult to say no even if it's not possible and would end up saying, 'Yes,' leaving you high and dry after two weeks. So a better question to the Japanese and the Chinese would be: 'When is the earliest you can deliver?'

Cognitive vs affective

Different cultures have different basis for trust: cognitive and affective.

The Americans, Australians, Brits and Germans are more likely to develop business relationships based on cognitive trust, or trust that comes from the head. These cultures place value on accomplishments, skills and reliability.

On the other hand, the Middle East, the Mediterranean region, Southeast Asia, Africa and the BRIC countries are guided by affective trust, or trust that stems from the heart. They place value on empathy, friendliness and emotional closeness.

So, to gain trust from the Americans and Germans, speak about your achievements and qualifications, and to gain trust of the Arabs and Indians, you must be friendly and have a personal connect.

I have a Dutch friend who has been living in Hong Kong for years and he consults various American firms on how to do business with the Chinese. According to him, you may have a duly signed 200-page agreement but that holds very little value compared to their word. It takes time to build trust with the Chinese, but that is the most important element in a fruitful business relationship. You need to pay attention to something called *guanxi*, which refers to one's connections or networks. Guanxi tends to be reciprocal in nature. Developing and maintaining guanxi involves conscious efforts, such as buying your client or vendor lunch, sending them gifts or socializing.

Written vs oral

Americans and Anglo-Saxons depend heavily on the written word, while Africans and Asians tend to prioritize oral communication. A Nigerian colleague, who, after finishing her call with her American colleague, received an email on the same matter. She felt offended that whatever was discussed was put into writing.

An Indian friend of mine was interviewing candidates for a particular position. She was impressed with the way an American expatriate fared in an interview and was all set to hire her. However, after the interview, she received an email from the candidate, who also copied everyone who had interviewed her, reiterating her enthusiasm for the role. My friend interpreted this as desperation and lack of trust and started having second thoughts about hiring this candidate.

The Cultural Table: A Summary

Nature	Meaning	Region
High vs Low Context	**High Context:** Use signals, gestures and norms **Low Context:** Are explicit in their words	**HC:** India, China, Japan and the Arab world **LC**: Americans and Anglo-Saxon countries
Upgraders vs Downgraders	**Upgraders:** Use words like 'totally', 'completely' and 'absolutely' **Downgraders**: Use words like 'partially', 'little bit' and 'maybe'	**U:** Russia, France, Germany and the Netherlands **D:** Mexico, Thailand, Japan, Peruvia, Middle East, India and Southeast Asia
Expressive vs Contained	**Expressive**: Comfortable showing emotion to others **Contained**: Not comfortable showing emotions to others	**E:** Brazil, France, Mexico, Saudi, India and the Philippines **C:** Denmark, Germany, the Netherlands, the UK, Sweden and Korea

Cognitive vs Affective	**Cognitive:** Trust is based on accomplishments, skills and reliability **Affective:** Trust based on empathy, friendliness and emotional closeness	**C:** America, Australia, the UK and Germany **A:** The Middle East, Mediterranien, BRIC, Southeast Asia and Africa
Written vs Oral	**W:** Depend heavily on the written word **O:** Depend heavily on the spoken word	**W:** America and the UK **O:** Indians, Africans, Arabs and Asians

Conclusion

By being aware of the nuances of different cultures, you stand a far greater chance of striking it off well with them and taking the negotiations to a much better level. In negotiations, culture has the potential of eating bargaining strategies for breakfast, lunch and dinner.

Chapter challenge: Cultural detective

Identify three friends or contacts you have on social media from three different countries. Ask them open-ended questions on three values: respect, freedom and equality. As you come to see how these values play out very differently for each culture, you will be in a far better position to empathize with them and be aligned with their culture so you can negotiate better.

Chapter 12

Negotiation Styles

Different Strokes for Different Folks

Whenever we face any conflict (seemingly incompatible concerns) or negotiation, each of us tend to act differently along two human dimensions of assertiveness and cooperation, i.e. we want to achieve our objective while at the same time, we have an obligation to support the other party in achieving their objective. Based on these two conflicting areas, there are five styles that a negotiator can fall under, as illustrated in the Thomas Kilmann matrix on the next page.

The Turtle: Avoiding

Turtles try to avoid conflicts and prefer to stay in the protective zone of their shells. They give up their personal goals and relationships. They stay away from the issues over which the conflict is taking place and from the people that they are in conflict with. They believe it is easier to withdraw (physically and psychologically) from a conflict than to face it.

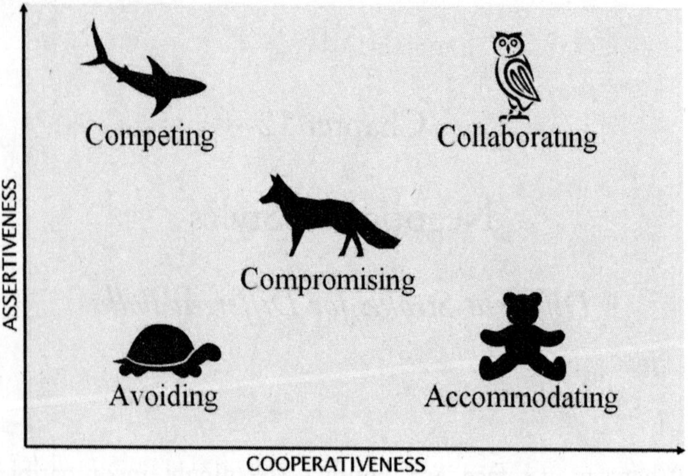

It could seem that the turtle doesn't care for either substance or relationships. However, it could be a good strategy when:

- Our needs can be met without negotiating.
- The ends are not worth the effort of a full-blown negotiation.
- There is more than one acceptable solution without having to negotiate at all.

An example of a situation when we must be a turtle: I am buying a car and I get the first price from the seller and realize it is ridiculous. I try to nudge the seller, but he seems a bit tough. I simply withdraw like the turtle for two simple reasons. There are a hundred other sellers in the market offering the same brand and model at a much cheaper rate. Second, I am not in any dire need to close the deal soon.

Being a turtle can also sometimes help overcome personal conflicts. My friend believes that it's important to sleep eight hours a day. I believe it depends on the state of mind; if I am stable and calm, four hours is enough. I understand his viewpoint and let go, and don't argue, although I may hold on to my understanding. I respect his point of view without imposing mine on him. Turtle style!

So you choose the battles you want to fight: if it ain't worth it, simply move on.

The Shark: Competing

Sharks try to overpower opponents by forcing them to accept their solution to the conflict. Their goals are highly important to them and the relationship is of minor importance. They seek to achieve their goals at all costs. The needs and approval of the other person are secondary. Sharks assume that the pie is fixed and they want to win it, giving them a sense of pride and achievement. Losing makes them feel weak, inadequate and more of a failure. They try to win by attacking, overpowering, overwhelming and intimidating other persons.

It may appear like the shark only cares for themselves, although it is a great strategy in these situations:

- Your interest in a good outcome is overwhelming, that is, it is more important than maintaining an ongoing relationship.

- It is a fixed-pie situation where either you get what you want, or the other party does.
- It is a one-off negotiation.

My colleagues may try to convince me of a choice which may seem favourable for all. I do realize that their thinking stems from fear, insecurity and even arrogance. I know that the choice I have made is based on my core values and purpose. I explain my choice, but they seem attached to their side. I then play the role of a shark. While their relationship is important to me, I use my purpose to guide my decisions.

You thus play the shark when you hold on to something very dear to you or invaluable that you do not want to give up at any cost.

Playing a shark does not necessarily mean that we must do so at the cost of relationships. I have seen families where a member has clearly demarcated certain time zones when they want to do certain activities and they have the agreement from others that they will not be disturbed during that time. In return, other members get to choose certain activities and time zones when they receive cooperation from the rest. If disturbed during their allotted times, I have seen them become sharks to protect their interest.

The Bear: Accommodating

To bears (more like huggable teddies), relationships are of great importance while their own goals are of little importance. Bears want to be accepted and liked by people (that is why the teddies). Their limiting belief is that conflicts cannot be discussed without damaging relationships. They are afraid that if conflict continues, someone will get hurt and that would ruin the relationship. Bears say, 'I'll give up my goals and let you have what you want in order for you to like me.' Bears try to smooth over the conflict in fear of harming the relationship.

Playing 'bear' is a good style when:

- Preserving or enhancing the relationship is very important.
- You are willing to lose in order to maintain the relationship.
- You will be negotiating over a period of time for a number of things.

I remember when I was in the business of waste management and we received a contract from TECOM for their first four buildings of Internet City in Dubai. Only four buildings, not so much of a big deal. They had some peculiar demands. They wanted us to provide them with smaller recycling bins for each floor of those buildings, appropriately marked for recycling. The cost of these were not included in our proposal; still I remember convincing my boss to agree, knowing that these guys would one day be so big that we might not be able to cater to their needs. That was one of the best decisions we made. The business soon grew; they expanded their facilities from Internet City to Media City and then to Knowledge Village. The size of the contract grew tenfold. I played the role of a 'bear' with the Emirati gentleman who was responsible for managing TECOM's facilities.

Becoming the huggable teddy sometimes pays off. I am a big believer in nurturing long-term relationships. I have had clients come to me after several years just because of this attitude. To summarize in favour of the bears: there is a word in Hindi, i.e. *baazigar*, where you lose the small stakes only to win the big ones.

The Fox: Compromising

Foxes are moderately concerned with their own goals and their relationships with other people. Foxes seek compromise. They give up part of their goals and persuade the other person in a conflict to give up part of his goals. They seek the easiest way in order to find agreement for the common ground.

This is a good style if:

- You are seeking a quick and easy end to a negotiation.
- The solution is intended to distribute resources or other items of value.
- It is difficult to decide whether to compete or accommodate.

Two partners start a business and contribute equal capital. Although the value of contribution of each partner may vary vastly, just to keep things simple, they agree to share profits equally.

I wish to go to the beach at 6 a.m. for a swim and my colleague wants to go there at 8 a.m. We settle for 7 a.m.

This style gets used in many places: neither my way, nor yours; let's settle for something in the middle—the easiest way out!

The Owl: Collaborating

We've saved the best for the last. Owls highly value their own goals as well as their relationships. They view conflicts as problems to be solved and seek a solution that achieves both their own goals and the goals of the other person in the conflict. Owls see conflicts as improving relationships by reducing tension between two people. They try to begin a discussion that identifies the conflict as a problem. By seeking solutions that satisfy both their own selves and the other party, owls maintain their relationships. Owls are not satisfied until a solution is found—one that helps achieve their goals as well as those of the other person's, and they are not satisfied until the tension and negative feelings have been fully resolved.

You should adopt the owl style of negotiation when:

- The outcome is just as important as the relationship.
- You need to do more than just split the difference, to ensure everyone is satisfied.
- You have the time required to find creative solutions that meet both parties' needs.

We are three colleagues living together. One of us has some peculiar habits that disturb the others, due to which we plan to begin living separately. We, however, in the most tactful way, convey the same to this person in order to see how he can make a few adjustments and introduce a few internal shifts in our set-up at home so that we do not get disturbed, and we continue living together. The owl is the wisest of all types.

We must begin any negotiation with the owl mindset. We must set off seeking mutual gain. It is only when we are restrained in some way or another should we settle for the other styles.

Conclusion

Be familiar with your dominant style and understand that if you go with that single style into every conflict or negotiation, you are bound to lose in the long term. Once you are aware of your style, understand the benefits of the other styles and the situations where they must be used. Thereafter, choose appropriately.

Chapter challenge: Shifting paradigms

Consider negotiations that you regularly have with someone where you have either been a shark (competing) or a bear (accommodating). Challenge yourself to be an owl the next time you get to negotiate with that same person. Record the new perspectives this brings.

Chapter 13

Closing the Deal

Consensus Building and Effective Agreements

A few years ago, we did a great job in negotiating a two-year project: favourable to our company and equally favourable to the client. I was super excited and returned to my office to share the big news with my colleagues. The contract reached me the next morning. We countersigned it and sent it back to the client. The project commenced. After fifteen days, when it was time for us to collect the payment, the client stated that we had extended them a forty-five-day credit period. We refused, saying fifteen days was our policy. However, when we rechecked our contract, we noticed that the client had silently amended the payment terms from fifteen days to forty-five days. Our team did not negotiate the payment terms and was only focusing on the overall amount and scope, and hence we overlooked this amendment.

A deal is never closed until we have covered all the bases, studied the contract with a fine-toothed comb, and dotted the i's and crossed the t's. A little hard work in this final phase ensures the negotiation achieves its desired result.

Closing a negotiation can mean two different things:

1. Building a consensus of different ideas: One of them could simply ask, 'Then, do we consider the deal closed?' They can orally spell out the terms, shake hands and come to a mutual agreement.
2. Formalize an agreement: This could take the shape of a signed contract or purchase order.

An effective negotiator pays attention both to building consensus and formalizing an agreement.

Implications of the agreement and building consensus

To demonstrate the importance of paying attention to building consensus and the value of thinking through the clauses in an agreement, I had organized a quick auction in one of my live sessions for a Dh.50 note (UAE Dirham). I fished out a Dh.50 note from my wallet, displayed it to the audience and told them that I was going to auction that currency note. Placing it on the desk, I clearly announced, 'This is going to be like every other auction where the highest bidder gets to keep the note and pays me the amount they bid. Nevertheless, we have one simple alteration to the usual auction. The second highest bidder will also pay the amount that they bid for, however they get nothing in return.' The auction started at Dh.10, with increments of Dh.5. Everyone was excited and the bidding began. Most of them were happy to bid all the way to Dh.50, but after that, there was an awkward silence. They did not know that there might be someone in the room who would be willing to pay anything above this, and they would all be proved wrong. At this stage, we had the highest bidder at Dh.50 and the second highest at Dh.45. The second highest bidder realized, at that moment, that he had to part with Dh.45 and leave without anything. He got restless and wanted to save his Dh.45. Thus he bid for Dh.55, believing his loss would be reduced. Now a tense competition between the top two bidders built up. Initially, they wanted to reduce their loss as much as they could and once they started reaching the levels of Dh.75 and Dh.80, they wanted to do everything to be the highest bidder so that they at least took the Dh.50 note and saved face.

Whenever I conduct this experiment with my business students or corporate clients, I have always ended up with the final bid in excess of Dh.100 and the participants are shocked that this could ever happen.

The devil is in the detail: The moment the participants found an alteration to the usual auction where 'the second bidder gets nothing but still pays', they should have realized that the deal was tilted in my favour and that should have raised flags. They should not have participated or not gone beyond Dh.25. This would have only been possible if they had paid full attention to the words spoken and not simply jumped into the game, believing it was another usual auction.

When finalizing any negotiation, this is perhaps the most important aspect to be considered.

Formalizing an agreement

Formalizing an agreement takes a special skill—the ability to translate generalities into specifics, scoping the responsibilities of each party, spelling out legalities, contract tenure, exclusions and so on. Bargaining is over at this stage of the process, although some negotiators may want to negotiate till the very end.

The agreement must be a **fair and accurate interpretation** of the consensus the parties have reached. While the basic agreement reached in the negotiation room will be the headline and what sticks in people's minds, it needs to be backed up with details of what, how, when and who. A smart negotiations team will have at least one 'detail's person' with them who is able to get the small print in place after the negotiators have put the outline in front of them.

Specific is terrific

When the terms of an agreement are not clearly spelt out, huge damage can be caused to either or both parties. Two employees may agree on their individual responsibilities for updating their company's website and a week could go by with nothing happening. The reason: there was no specificity as to who would have to begin and by when.

All essential terms, along with the practicalities of implementation, must be clearly stated in writing. The agreement that emerges at the end of the negotiation must particularly spell out **the 'how' factor**. At the initial stages of the negotiation, the what, when and how emerge. The 'how' is the most important of all, as without the firm details of the how, you leave things open to individual assumptions.

During my tenure at the 'waste management' company, we had an agreement signed with a prestigious five-star hotel in Dubai. We agreed to collect the garbage from their premises and transport it to the landfill. We assumed our team was responsible for the garbage once it reached outside the hotel into the skips and the hotel assumed that we were responsible to collect all individual bins that were inside the hotel too. A big mess-up ensued owing to the fact that we did not specify who would do what.

Calling it quits

Negotiations have the potential of getting heated and even getting out of hand. While negotiations need not necessarily be a very friendly process, we need to keep personal conflicts and unfair tactics from interfering with the process.

It is absolutely okay to call it quits when:

- You feel threatened or extremely uncomfortable.
- You sense unfair tactics.

Walking away from a negotiation is not always a sign of defeat, especially when you strongly feel that things are going south because the other party is crossing the line. Putting an end to a meeting with an invitation to reconvene at a later date may sometimes be the best thing to do. Sometimes you may notice the other party uses tactics that are threatening so as to put your confidence and patience to the test. They do this because they have seen it work in the past and expect it to work every time. You could, however, put your foot down when you notice such unacceptable behaviour, sending a signal to the other party that you will not be intimidated or treated that way. Once they understand that you cannot be taken for granted, their behaviour changes. When negotiations go off track and one party starts playing foul, they never bear good results for either one.

Some battles are better lost than won

A prestigious client of ours was the operator of a huge container port in the UAE. It took us great efforts to bag that contract. They had contracted manpower to secure cargo for the transportation of containers. A few months down the line, our workers were being abused by the supervisors onsite. When I escalated this to the port operations head, he virtually 'gave a damn'. The tipping point came when the operations head himself started behaving in a very contemptuous manner with all our personnel. We did escalate this to the CEO of the group but realized that his hands were tied too as the port operations head was specially recommended by their biggest client (a container carrier). Having tried all options and failing, we gave them a three-month notice and withdrew all our men from the site. We knew that continuing to work there would only add to the humiliation of our people, and in business, unless there is mutual respect, is there a point in continuing?

Conclusion

Close a negotiation with as much fervour as you had during the opening and bargaining phases. Look to solicit consensus on a definite conclusion. Formalize an agreement based on the consensus, spelling out specifically every detail of the roles, responsibilities, terms and conditions. At any point of time if you feel threatened, call it quits.

Chapter challenge: A fine-toothed comb

The next time you come to terms with or have an agreement with someone, check if you have covered all the bases, i.e. the what, how, who, when and where. Run through each of these in detail and you will have the clearest agreement ever.

Chapter 14

Your First Job Negotiation

Maximizing Value from the Start

When I met Malaykaa Malhotra last month, she was excited that she had landed her first job with a reputable company. As we conversed about her role, I checked if she had negotiated the salary offered to her and she said, 'Well, it was my first job, hence I took whatever I was offered.' This is a classic mistake many first-timers make and rightly so. While there is ample anxiety surrounding the first job, where the priority is to get relevant experience in the field of interest, there is more we can do to negotiate.

Why negotiate the first offer?

- The prospective employer usually has a range to offer, and rarely offers the maximum in their first offer.

They have a cushion and will be more than willing to stretch if nudged.

- Your stating salary has a huge impact on the trajectory of your earnings. It becomes a benchmark for all future increments within the company and when changing jobs.
- When done well, your prospective employer has a good impression of you. You are recognized as someone who is assertive and has the skill to claim value—an asset to any organization in the long term.
- When you negotiate, you enhance the outcome for both parties. Besides salary, you could negotiate the job role, perks, working environment, performance indicators and so on. This way, you set things up in a way that will contribute to your best performance, and hence better results for the company.

Difference between negotiating for the first job interview and future job interviews

- Anxiety: In the first interview, you are far more anxious than in your second or third interview. This anxiety may work against your confidence.
- Experience: You are less experienced, hence need to read much more and be far more prepared in your first interview. This may even work to your advantage because you can negotiate well from a space of innocence and let your prospective employer know that you don't have the greatest negotiation skills although you are applying some best practices.

- Anticipation: A good negotiator would anticipate various moves of the interviewer and be prepared with appropriate turns. For a first-timer, this would be quite difficult to do.
- BATNA: You have a weak BATNA in your first interview, unless you already have another offer that is as good or better than the one you are interviewing for. When you are interviewing for your second job, you usually have your existing job as a strong BATNA to fall back upon.
- Corporate competence: There is a huge gap between theory and practice. In your first interview, you may have read and heard about how corporates and teams work, but in reality, you may not have had the real feel and this could be an area of concern.
- Technical competence: You have amazing scores in college/university to brag about, but that may not be enough to give you the best deal in your first interview. The prospective company is looking for practical experience, and hence your internships, voluntary involvement in relevant projects and practical work in the field must be highlighted for brownie points.

Preparing for your first job interview

The three most important words in any negotiation: prepare, prepare and prepare. While preparation before the interview impresses the interviewer as evidence that you are serious about the position, it also gives you an upper hand when it comes to how well you negotiate. Here are a few things that we must be prepared with:

- Company profile: You must know the business of your prospective employer. Thoroughly research their products and services, their history, current operations, recent achievements and future goals. Delve deeper to understand their reputation as employers and anticipate how much they would be willing to offer you for the position applied.
- The industry: Try to understand the industry in which the company operates, especially in terms of the average salaries being offered for similar positions.
- BATNA: Have you interviewed elsewhere? Do you have other offers as yet? Are you speaking to other employers? What is your 'employment' pipeline looking like? Finding answers to these questions will help you in figuring out your BATNA and hence will give you a good indication of your 'Walk-away Price'. Additionally, anticipating and knowing their BATNA will help you understand your demand and will make your position stronger.
- Job description: Try to understand the role, the required skills and, more importantly, the value it brings to the company. A good negotiator claims higher value when they can create high value for the other party.
- Questions: Interviewers like powerful questions and would appreciate your asking relevant and structured questions when asked to do so. It shows that you have done your homework and that you are analytical. All these traits can stack up in your favour during the negotiation.
- Interviewers: Building rapport with the interviewer in the first few minutes of the interview is an important

negotiation strategy. Getting to know the names of the members of the interviewing panel, looking them up on LinkedIn and building associations that may be worthy of pointing out during the interview will be invaluable. All things being equal, interviewers hire those that they like (and usually they like those that are like them).

- Mental composure: Before getting into the interview, you have a great deal to work on your 'mind' to keep it free from unwanted emotions and to fill it with positivity, power and gratitude. Remember, you carry your attitude with you wherever you go, and preparing this way will be invaluable.

Maximizing value during the interview

- Rapport and trust: Connect with your interviewers at a personal level. Match and mirror their body language in the best possible way. Unconsciously, they feel you are like them, and they start liking you. First impressions really matter. Next, your honesty, transparency and an attitude of vulnerability will build 'affective' trust. Displaying your credentials, achievements and qualifications will build 'cognitive' trust.
- Effective communication: Empathetic listening to know what is expected before presenting or offering how you can be of value is important.
- Showcasing skills, abilities and achievements with respect to expectations: This will give you a good chance to prove the value you can bring to the table once you join.

- Confidence: While you could bear a confident demeanour in general, a large part of your confidence while negotiating will depend on your BATNA.
- Your uniqueness: Being self-aware will support you in bringing out your unique selling proposition. It is perfectly okay to share your shortcomings as long as you can have them overshadowed by your strengths and you have plans in place to overcome them or work around them.
- Emotional poise: Interviewers are keen to know how emotionally intelligent you are. While you may be hired largely in the capacity of an individual contributor, they will be keen to see how well you will work with a team, and whether you have the qualities to lead teams. A large part of this will depend on your emotional intelligence. One negotiation principle useful here is 'separate person from problem', and by applying this, you will create clarity of distance and be in a much better position to understand where they are coming from.
- Use standards: When negotiating for better salary, perks, hybrid working (home and office), health benefits and so on, it is good to refer acceptable and relevant standards or industry practices. This strengthens your position dramatically.
- Move away from positions and focus on interest: Whenever making a demand, it is important to share your inhibitions or desires behind that demand. The company may have alternative ways to cater to them. In the same way, whenever they take a stand on something, request them to explain their interests so that you may provide alternatives.

- Generate options: Bring every bit of your creative capacity to the interview. Have various alternatives that would support a win-win for you and the company. Think on behalf of both. For example, when you are told that you may not have the flexibility to work from home, and you understand that the reason for this is to maximize teamwork and efficiency, be ready to offer five other ways for the company to have great teamwork and efficiency despite WFH options.

Anticipate moves and manoeuvre turns

As a strategy to negotiate hard, interviewers try to undermine the qualifications and value the candidate brings to the table. These are called 'moves'. As an antidote to moves, the candidate can come prepared with 'turns', which not only neutralize the moves but capitalize on them and convert them into opportunities.

The following chart indicates possible moves by the interviewers and suggested turns that the candidates can take.

MOVES (by the interviewer)	**TURNS (by the candidate)**
You are a fresher.	I am free from any baggage, bring a fresh mindset, will easily fit in and am a quick learner.
We will be spending ample time and energy in training you.	The more I learn, the more I will contribute to the organization.

You will get the expected salary only when we are satisfied with your performance.	We could mutually agree on a starting salary. With clear performance indicators, I am confident about my performance and hence am willing to work out on increments based on my performance with specific timelines. I am sure if I exceed expectations, my salary will be proportionately increased.
I have seen many candidates who are willing to settle for less than what you are demanding.	I can speak for myself. I understand the value I will bring to the organization. Based on that, I am making a reasonable request.
You do have the technical skills, but it will take you time to develop the soft skills required for this role.	I have been involved with many projects and extracurricular activities. I have worked effectively with others and always succeeded in achieving the goals set.
It will become a precedent and hence we cannot offer anything higher.	I am sure you will not set a precedent for anyone less deserving. Thus, this kind of a precedent would assure you of the best of talent.

The Big Q: What is your expected salary?

An interviewer who puts such a question to the candidate does not perhaps know the effect of anchoring. If this question hitherto made candidates nervous, be assured this is the best opportunity to negotiate in their favour. Research has proved that if given a choice, be the one to make the opening offer. Additionally, place a high figure and support it with a plausible reference or standard. By doing so, you are 'anchoring' the other party and the negotiation would usually end at a point closer to the anchored figure.

Unfortunately, I have seen candidates avoid this question with a counter-question: 'Well, is there a budget that you have?' or 'I am willing to go with what you have to offer as I am a fresher and do not have an idea of the market.' A good way to answer this question would be: 'Thank you for asking me this question. I have done some research within the industry with respect to this role and position. I believe "Rs ABC" is a fair pay. In fact, one of my batchmates was recently hired by a similar organization for the same pay.'

Once you have confidently and calmly landed your amount and supported it with a relevant standard, give a pause and allow the interviewer to respond. Avoid trying to be defensive or over-justifying it.

Now—Probation—Future: It will be good to speak about your salary in three parts. My current expectation, what I would expect upon confirmation after probation and annual reviews to cover for inflation/industry/needs.

Things to avoid

- Asking if the salary is negotiable: There is no point in asking this question because we must understand that everything is negotiable. The best thing to do is to start negotiating on the salary and other benefits. By asking if the salary is negotiable, we corner the interviewer and leave them with two choices: yes or no. If they say no, we are stuck. If they say yes, they get stuck. They would usually wiggle out and get you stuck even if they know that the salary was, in fact, negotiable.

- Saying that you are open for negotiations: I have seen candidates who put forward their demand and then say, 'I am open for negotiations.' This creates an image that what you have just said was a bluff. You had something much lesser in mind.
- Saying something like, 'I am expecting Rs 20,000–25,000: Give them a single figure. A range means that you are ready for anything between Rs 20,000 and Rs 25,000. The interviewer will obviously take Rs 20,000 and ignore the Rs 25,000, which was in this case redundant. It is always better to specify the amount. Let them figure out the range.

Being before doing

There were times when companies hired for skills and fired for attitude. This resulted in massive employee turnover within the first eighteen months of hiring. It was found that while candidates were skilled enough, they simply failed in their attitude. Companies are now smart. They not only look for relevant skills, but they have included various processes to understand a candidate's attitude before hiring.

Here are a few things to keep in mind that will enhance your 'being' self.

- Be presentable: Dress as you would on an important day. It passes a strong message on your disposition to this company you are interviewing for.

- Be punctual: Unless you have had unavoidable circumstances like Chris Gardner (played by Will Smith in *The Pursuit of Happyness*), who was thrown into jail for not paying a parking ticket and reached late for his interview, covered in paint and without a shirt. He pulled off the interview very well with his presence of mind. When Chris gets asked, 'What would you say if a guy walked in for an interview without a shirt on, and I hired him?' his response was natural, humorous and very appropriate given the situation: 'He must have had some really nice pants on!'
- Be grateful: You have been given an opportunity and others are taking time out to assess your capabilities. Be genuinely grateful, it will show in your words and actions.
- Be gracious: This includes being polite, respectful and courteous. There is a good chance of you getting overwhelmed by the interview process or you becoming a bit too familiar with the interviewer and going overboard. Keep your gracious guard up always; you will be proud of yourself.

A departing note

All's well that ends well. This holds true in your interview. Here are some thoughts that will support you just before you depart:

- Have a good amount of relevant questions to ask if you did not get that opportunity before.

- Understand when they will revert to you. If you do not hear back from them, ask how and who you can contact.
- Thank the interviewer(s) for the opportunity to be interviewed. Let them know that you look forward to working in their company.
- Send a note of thanks to the panel/contact person post the interview (within one working day).

Chapter challenge: Best foot forward

Your preparation for your first job interview will support you in negotiating a better deal for yourself. In the chapter we have discussed various moves that you can anticipate from the interviewer and the appropriate turns that you can consider. In addition, it would be useful for you to contemplate on some open-ended questions that will strengthen your position. Here is a list of five such questions that help interviewers size you up. Be creative while considering responses to these questions yet be genuine and honest.

1. Why should we hire you?
2. How do you manage anxiety and stress?
3. What is one poor habit you would like to overcome?
4. How would you define success?
5. What questions do you have for us?

Chapter 15

Navigating Internal Negotiations

Strategies for Career Growth at the Workplace

The impact of negotiating salaries can be astounding. According to Linda C. Babcock, a leading expert in negotiations and the James M. Walton Professor of economics at Carnegie Mellon, a one-time salary negotiation can land you $627,000 over a lifetime.

You might be thinking—well, what would I have to do to get that extra amount? You might even suspect that it was either illegal or dangerous. Actually, it's none of those. All you need to do is negotiate. So let's see how this would work.

Take two people graduating from college today at age twenty-two. We will call them Girish and Bose and let's say that they both get equal job offers. Girish takes the offer, but Bose decides to negotiate, and he gets the offer raised by 10 per cent. Let's take these two as they go through their careers until they retire at sixty-five. Let's assume that they each get a 3 per cent raise every year. Now, if we think about how much more money Bose made over Girish, if Bose took the extra money from negotiating and put it in a savings account. By the time they are sixty-five, Bose would have $627,354 in that account. So you can think about it this way, that that amount of money is the return on a one-time negotiation.

The numbers may look unrealistic, but that is the power of compounding. We may think that a 10 per cent salary hike does not translate to much, so we should take whatever we are offered. But if we do the math with respect to the compounding of interest and consider the fact that organizations usually calculate increments on the base salary, we will wake up to preparing before those interviews and sharpen our negotiation skills, no matter what!

Salary negotiations during interviews is one thing and ongoing salary negotiations at the workplace is another. I believe that we are quite smart in negotiating during recruitment interviews and I cannot overemphasize the importance of being honest here. We do not have to be dishonest to get the best deal for us. Remember, every recruiter has a salary range to manoeuvre with; besides, they have a host of benefits that they would be willing to offer to the right candidate, provided we know how to ask. I have been on interview panels and hired candidates across every level in the organization. While we have tried to maintain uniformity across the board, sometimes we have given away a great deal more to candidates than we had initially anticipated. As a candidate, it is vital to first impress the interviewer about your knowledge, skills and attitude of a position and then to bring forth the salary/benefit negotiations.

Let's consider the things that we need to be aware of in ongoing negotiations within the workplace.

Complexity in internal negotiations

Internal negotiations are complex and include additional dynamics that may not exist in negotiations that happen outside the organization. Listed below are some of the unique aspects of negotiating internally:

- People know you: Your reputation precedes you and hence the negotiation begins much before you know of it. There is plenty of work you do to build your case ahead of the negotiation.
- People know the subject: Nothing is hidden really. You do not have the luxury of withholding information that may be a deterrent to you. Things are quite transparent and you must learn to work around such transparency.
- Internal politics: Despite managing the entire negotiation process as skilfully as possible, there are many factors that may determine the outcome that are beyond your control.
- Organizational policies: These are additional barriers that restrict the scope of negotiations, while at the same time they could work favourably. Knowing these policies thoroughly and interpreting them

accurately would be a big advantage. Additionally, keeping a tab on precedent relevant to the subject would also be supportive.

- Personal prejudices: Being in the good books of the decision makers always works in your favour. To attain this, some may go out of their way to please others, but demonstrating the simple human values of respect and cooperation can work wonders too.
- Reputation retention: You tend to continue meeting the 'other party' on a daily basis regardless of how the negotiation goes. It is hence critical that professional behaviour is displayed throughout the process and bridges are not burnt even if the outcome was not in your favour. What you do sets a precedent. Hence, upholding your reputation is crucial.

Our disposition to authority

A great deal of negotiations within organizations happen with our seniors and those who hold positions of authority. Even before we understand how we approach such negotiations, it is critical to decipher our internal construct with reference to authority. Our internal construct plays a very subtle but immensely powerful role in the entire negotiation process.

There are three types of dispositions to authority, and we may fall under any one of these:

- Mutual disposition: I need you as much as you need me. We both need each other equally while acknowledging the fact that the superior has more powers.

- Counter dependence (Aversion to authority): I dislike authority and cannot stand you as a superior.
- Over dependence (The leader is all-knowing): The tendency to agree with everything that authority says/does. The Milgram Experiment, named after Stanley Milgram, conducted a relevant experiment to show how people comply with perceived experts (and people with authority), even to the point of personal distress. It was shocking to note that human beings are very gullible to 'perceived' authority, even when they know that the person with that authority is incorrect.

Do some soul-searching and analyse what your disposition is to authority. Over dependence and counter dependence will work against you in negotiations. Should you be prone to these, it is important that you first begin work here. Aversion comes when you hold deep negative beliefs around authority. Try to understand the root and release it with the realization that authority is vital for flow of communication, command and decision-making. On the other hand, over dependence comes when you do not appreciate your role enough. You look up to your superior as someone who is actually 'superior' instead of someone who has a superior title and position 'organizationally'. You must respect that position as much as you respect yours, otherwise you would avoid negotiations or would allow yourself to be treated like a doormat, taking everything lying down. Your endeavour must be to get to a space of 'mutual dependence', where you deeply realize that you both need each other equally.

Once we have our disposition in place, we are safe to negotiate with our boss. It may not necessarily be with salary hikes or promotions alone. We may want to negotiate on various aspects such as the type of work, location, timing, flexibility, approving innovative ideas and so on.

Managing my manager

Internal negotiations are far simpler than we usually expect. We must bear in mind only three determining factors in our negotiation. These are:

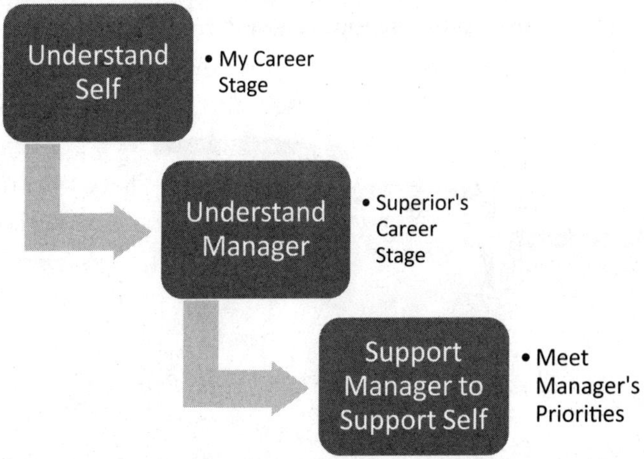

Understand Self and Understand Manager: It is important to know what stage I am in my career and at what stage my boss is in. Only when I know the stage both of us are in can I clearly think of my boss's priorities and help them get what they want so that eventually they help me get what I want (a win-win).

Career stage

Our career stage depends on various factors such as tenure in the company, tenure in the department, change in job role, change in the team members, change in work location and so on. Both the self and the manager go through similar career stages; at any given point, they may be at the same level or at different levels. Even if both are on the same level, what they will need from each other will be very different.

The following are the four stages in a person's career:

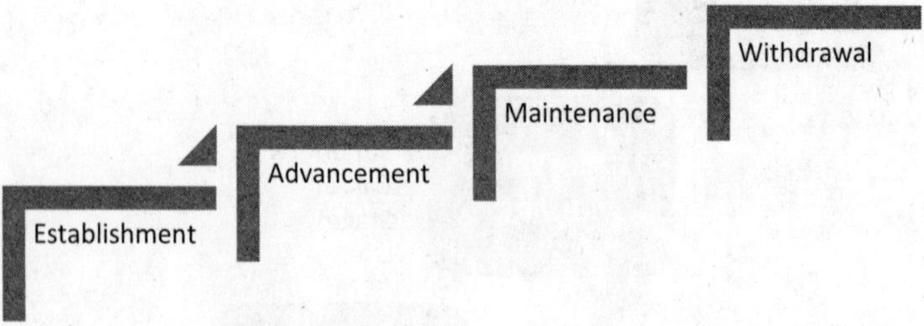

Lloyd Baird and Kathy Kram, Career Dynamics

The following table outlines the different needs of the employee and the leader, corresponding to different stages in their careers:

Career stage	Needs of the employee	Needs of the leader
Establishment	Develop competence and build confidence	Demonstrate managerial competence and learn how things work
Advancement	Promotion and growth	Make a name for self
Maintenance	Autonomy and contribution	Sharing wisdom and developing others
Withdrawal	Consultative role and acknowledgement	Consultative role and acknowledgement

When I was a sales executive closing deal after deal for my company, I was progressing quickly through the advancement stage. My manager then was at the maintenance stage, where he was more than willing to share his wisdom and mentor me. I recognized that and informally accepted him as my mentor. He would be so happy seeing me learn from him and seek his input and feedback on various matters related to sales and management. When I knew I was ready, I asked him for a larger role and he more than willingly referred me for an open position to the CEO and got me confirmed.

Anyone who wants to get the best from their manager or leader must have a clear understanding of their career needs. If, for example, you are at a maintenance stage, what you expect is autonomy. Having understood that, consider where your leader is and support them there. That way, they will feel fulfilled and be willing to support you in your needs and give you the space you need.

Moves and turns in internal negotiations

Moves and turns are a way of understanding what is happening in a negotiation as the parties deal with their issues. *Moves* are the actions negotiators take to position themselves (and others) in the negotiation process. *Turns* are the responses to the others' moves. In making moves, negotiators strive to present themselves as competent and legitimate, so as to maximize their influence over the process. They use strategic moves to position themselves advantageously, to have their take on the situation, thereby weakening the other's position. In other words, the moves of a negotiator can potentially unsettle or undermine the other party.

Below are examples of how the other party can say things or make moves that can put the negotiator on the defensive. So, if you are going to approach your boss to negotiate a raise, the following are moves you may want to anticipate:

- Challenge: 'I don't think you are ready for a raise as yet.'
- Undermine: 'I am surprised that you even considered yourself eligible for a raise.'
- Criticize: 'Ha, you still don't know how to leverage social media.'
- Threat: I still haven't told anyone about your fiasco with our biggest bank.'
- Flattery: 'You are one of the most understanding people on the team and you know this is not the right time for a raise.'

It is possible for your boss to make the above 'moves', thus putting you on the defensive. Your natural reaction would be for you to come up with a counter move, which is not the best alternative. For example, when they say, 'You are not yet ready for the promotion,' your counter move would be, 'But of course I am ready.' A counter move keeps you in the same defensive position. You however have better options to choose from, called 'turns'.

'Turns' are different from counter moves as they can reframe the situation. A turn can change the dynamics of the situation.

Five types of turns are useful:

- Interrupting: Interrupting the action disrupts the move. When you are told you are not yet ready, simply remain silent for a few moments and then continue. Doing so, you have disrupted their claim.
- Naming: To name a move signals recognition of what is occurring. It suggests that the negotiator is not affected by the threat. 'I sense a threat in your statement, and I will not let that stop me from asking what I deserve.'
- Questioning: Rather than directly naming a move, to question it is to throw it back to the 'mover' implying one is not sure what is prompted. 'What do you mean by a "fiasco" with our biggest client?"
- Correcting: A correcting turn substitutes a different version or motivation to the one the move implied. Rather than just rejecting what is said, a correcting turn offers a different explanation. 'While I am growing my social media knowledge, so far, I have received the largest number of leads through social media in our team.'

- Diverting: A diverting turn shifts the focus to the problem itself. It is a way of ignoring the implication of the move but also has the negotiator take control of the process. For example, somebody challenges your expertise: 'You don't know how to leverage social media.' A diverting turn might be: 'Let's see where we as a company stand when it comes to social media and understand some changes that will enhance our brand and push us forward.'

Steps that support stepping up

- Anticipate all possible moves and have logical responses and turns available for the moves.
- Carry records of milestones and achievements with supportive documentation relevant to Key Performance Indicators, objectives and expectations of the company.
- Carry records of testimonials, both internal and external.
- Have readily available data to support obstacles and challenges that you met.
- Have your calendar handy to fix future appointments instantly.
- Be organized and access the right information at the right time.
- Be fully aware of company policies and relevant procedures.
- Be fully aware of all recent changes in the company.
- Be available with information on achievements and support extended outside the regular course of work

that benefited and enhanced the reputation of your company, department and leader.

Your raise is guaranteed

According to Herb Cohen, a salary negotiation must not be abruptly held by the employee. It must be planned way in advance if it is to be successful.[10]

He suggests that an initial meeting be held between the employee and boss at the start of the year to understand expectations from both sides. Once done, it is important to come back to the table every quarter to understand if you as the employee are meeting those criteria. Then a final one at the end of the year where you can show with evidence what you have achieved. You cannot be too off the mark because of the structure you adopted.

Conclusion

The dynamics of internal negotiations may be different from the rest, but if we follow a logical approach, we can experience enrichment and fulfilment galore. Realize that the benefits from internal negotiations are humongous and with the right disposition to authority, you win the battle of the mind. You follow that up with enhanced career awareness of yourself and your leader and seek mutual gain.

[10] Herb Cohen's interview with Barry Nalebuff, 'Negotiating a Salary' (In the online course titled 'Introduction to Negotiation: A Strategic Playbook for Becoming a Principled and Persuasive Negotiator' by Yale University)

Chapter challenge: Managing up

Role playing a salary hike negotiation with your manager: Imagine that you are going to approach your manager for a salary hike. Write down your plan and prepare as you get ready for the negotiation.

Recruit a partner—someone who knows you well and who you can trust. Brief them on your work, your manager, the situation and have them role play the manager. Rehearse it several times.

That is, practise doing it several ways to see what works, what doesn't.

Debrief with your partner.

Have your partner tell you what worked and what didn't when rehearsing.

After that you might want to buy your partner a nice present.

Chapter 16

Negotiation Nuggets

Timeless Wisdom for Successful Deals

To help you strengthen your negotiation muscle, listed below is a rapid-fire of points that able negotiators use in various contexts. Even if you can fully understand and apply one of these points, your negotiation capability will instantly go up a notch!

Ten timeless thoughts on negotiation

1. Prepare, prepare and prepare: These are the three most important words in any negotiation.
2. Time your moves and empathize with different cultures: Have the power to change the face of any negotiation.

3. Ask and you shall receive: This goes with the classic maxim that you don't get what you deserve, you get what you negotiate for.
4. Ramp up your listening skills: Communication plays a key role in negotiation, and within that, listening plays the most crucial role.
5. Release your EGO: Ego is an emotion that can derail every negotiation; let it go before it closes all doors of opportunity.
6. Flex your stand: Understand what your interests are, look for interests in the other party (real needs, fears and aspirations) and find the best ways to fulfill them. Be flexible and don't dig yourself into 'a position'. A position is a stand you take on 'what you want'; however, there may be several ways of fulfilling it. Be open to those possibilities.
7. Offer and expect commitment: Every time we make a commitment that the other party expects of us, it is the best time to make them commit to something too. If they want a delivery within two days (which normally takes five days), then you can request that they make the payment in a day (which is normally done in a week).
8. Don't absorb their problems: We all have problems, and some negotiators try to play the victim and share their problems just so that the other party drops their guard. They might say something like: 'Owing to the pandemic, our business has been severely hit. We want a 50 per cent discount.' Observe and be empathetic without getting absorbed in their problem so your sense of discretion remains unaffected.

9. Stick to your principles: We like to look back and be proud of the things we have and our achievements. If we have compromised on our principles, something will keep haunting us till our graves (and perhaps beyond).
10. Close with a confirmation: Although the Japanese may say 'yes' and many others from my region nod their heads making one believe that they have a closure, it is important that we have things spelt out clearly. Ambiguity is a negotiator's worst enemy.

Ten tenacious techniques

1. Aim high: The problem with most negotiators is that they aim low and achieve their mark!
2. Avoid asking killer questions: Don't ask questions like: 'Is this your last offer?' 'Is the price negotiable?' (Everything is negotiable and the other party, just to save face, may be forced to fix themselves in their position.)
3. Beware of 'defence dropping' statements: Some smart negotiators like to paint an awful picture of themselves in order to gain the sympathy of the other party. 'I'm only a simple businessman,' they would say. Nevertheless, they may be highly successful, operating several other businesses and running a few bank accounts in Switzerland.
4. Challenge 'Mother Hubbards': When the other party shows you documents and evidence as proof that they are barely earning anything or that they have exhausted all their budgets, they are being 'Mother

Hubbards'. A lot more happens outside of the documents that are made visible to us, and we should not get carried away by their 'projected' transparency. Besides, budgets are merely guidelines and can be tweaked when we see great return on our investment.

5. Use assertive language: Include assertive words in your language such as 'I need', 'This is a must', 'Please' and 'I insist on it'.
6. Capitalize on non-verbals: You are never 'not communicating'. Body language and para-verbal (tone of voice) communication take up 93 per cent of our communication (research by Prof. Albert Mehrabian), so we need to 'bring our complete selves on'.
7. Make use of padding: All offers usually have a padding, i.e they have a range kept for negotiations. Remember this and never refrain from asking them to sweeten the deal for you.
8. Use 'what do you know?' So what do you know about the uniqueness of our services? What do you know about the market prices? What do you know about the durability of the product? What do you know about the other brand? Use these questions with caution as they must land politely once you have built a rapport.
9. Don't be trapped by 'Yesable' propositions: The negotiator asks a string of questions that are usually answered by a 'yes'. They tactfully insert a 'closing question' to seal the deal and anticipate a yes to that too. An example: Hope you are clear about the experience you will get when you deal with us? (Yes . . .), Did you see that you are saving at least

35 per cent if you sign up for the deal this month? (Yes . . .), Would you like that we begin your service tomorrow? (expect a Yes)

10. Enjoy nibbling: When the other party has invested a good amount of time and energy in negotiating a deal, it is easy to nibble at a few little extras just before finalizing it. Since the other party has already come so far, they would not drop the deal just for a few rupees more.

Ten reasons to demand for a discount

Payment related:

1. When making a payment on time
2. When making an early payment
3. When paying in advance
4. When placing an order before a date
5. When paying in a certain format (say, cash)

Stock-related:

1. When the stock is new (because you are the first to test those goods)
2. When the stock is old
3. When purchasing high volumes
4. When my order is incomplete (when I have ordered for twenty items and I receive only eighteen)
5. When my order is mistaken (when I have ordered for a classic model and I am delivered a variation of it)

Ten more reasons to demand a discount

Delivery-related:

1. Delivering at awkward times, such as out-of-office timings, midnight or public holidays
2. Rescheduling my delivery
3. Giving me instant delivery (because I am helping them save on their warehousing)
4. Delayed delivery
5. Missed my delivery
6. Incomplete or missed order

Goodwill/trust-related:

1. When giving permission to use your name on marketing material
2. As a reward for recommendation
3. For being loyal to the supplier
4. When placing all business with one supplier

Your negotiation gym: Six-week programme

There has been extensive research on factors that lead to great performance. Two things that always come up are the need for hard work and practice. Similar to the gym that we visit when we want to have a fit physique, we have curated a 'Negotiation Gym' for your development in the area of negotiations. It is a six-week programme that will get you honed.

Week one: Start out with some easy things. Engage in a negotiation that you think you can easily win, just to get warmed up. For example, at a restaurant, request for a brighter table, a better view, etc.

Week two: Stretch out, that is set some higher targets for yourself. Just push yourself a little bit more to ask for more. For example, ask the steward at the restaurant for something that is not on the menu. Request that you speak to the chef or manager personally to make sure your request is accepted.

Week three: I call this 'piling it on'. Just practise negotiating for things you think you actually don't deserve. For example, ask your cable provider to allow the viewing of a paid channel free for a week. Ask your neighbour to look after your plants when you are gone for a vacation (if they have never done so before).

Week four: Step it up. Just work a little harder, do some things that are a bit outside your comfort zone. If you have never spoken to a particular neighbour, reach out now.

Week five: Go long. Take some long shots, ask for some things that you think you might not get. Call a hotel in town and ask them for a staycation where you pay for one day and they pay for the next. Escalate that to the manager there if you are not entertained.

Week six: Actively court rejection. Keep asking until you hear a no. Why must you let go until you get a no? A no is actually a good sign. It means you have pushed the boundary a little bit. Because remember, if you've never heard a no, it means that you aren't asking for enough. For example, call a popular baker when someone has a birthday coming up. Let them know it is their birthday and have them send a cake to the birthday boy/girl free of cost.

Once you do this six-week programme, treat yourself to your favourite smoothie.